Stephanie Whitfeld

AIRMONT SHAKESPEARE CLASSICS SERIES

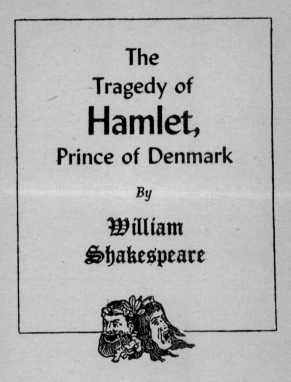

The
Tragedy of
Hamlet,
Prince of Denmark

By

William Shakespeare

AIRMONT PUBLISHING COMPANY, INC.
22 EAST 60TH STREET · NEW YORK 10022

PREFACE

For the Airmont series of plays by William Shakespeare, we have chosen a text that we believe more nearly preserves the flavor of the old Shakespearean English than do those of more modernized versions.

In a popular-priced paperback edition, it is almost impossible to include a complete compilation of notes because of the limitations of the format. We suggest that the reader refer to the following excellent textbooks for additional material: *The New Valiorum* (Cambridge and Arden editions); the Globe edition edited by W. G. Clark and W. A. Wright (1866); the Oxford edition edited by W. J. Craig (1891); and the editions by G. L. Kittredge (1936). Also, the following books will be helpful to a better understanding of Shakespeare: *Prefaces to Shakespeare, First Series* (London, 1933); John Palmer, *Political Characters of Shakespeare* (London, 1945); Gerald Sanders, *A Shakespeare Primer* (New York and Toronto, 1945); J. Dover Wilson, *The Essential Shakespeare* (London, 1930, New York, 1932).

Dr. David G. Pitt, who wrote the general introduction for each of the plays, received his B.A. degree from Mt. Allison University in New Brunswick, and his M.A. and Ph.D. degrees from the University of Toronto. Since 1949, he has been in the English Department at Memorial University of Newfoundland and Professor of English there since 1962. His publications include articles on literary and educational subjects, and editorial work on Shakespeare.

Gino J. Matteo, who wrote the introduction for *Hamlet*, received his B.A. at the University of Toronto in 1959 and his M.A. there in 1962. He is presently a Lecturer in the Department of English at St. Michael's College in the University of Toronto, and is now engaged in a Canada Council scholarship at the Folger Shakespeare Library in Washington, D.C., where he is completing a doctoral dissertation on the theatrical and literary history of Shakespeare's *Othello*.

GENERAL INTRODUCTION

William Shakespeare: His Life, Times, and Theatre

HIS LIFE

The world's greatest poet and playwright, often called the greatest Englishman, was born in Stratford-upon-Avon, Warwickshire, in the year 1564. The exact date of his birth is uncertain, but an entry in the *Stratford Parish Register* gives his baptismal date as April 26. Since children were usually baptized two or three days after birth, it is reasonable to assume that he was born on or about April 23—an appropriate day, being the feast of St. George, the patron saint of England.

His father, John Shakespeare, was a glover and dealer in wool and farm products, who had moved to Stratford from Snitterfield, four miles distant, some time before 1552. During his early years in Stratford his business prospered, enabling him to acquire substantial property, including several houses, and to take his place among the more considerable citizens of the town. In 1557 he married Mary, daughter of Robert Arden, a wealthy landowner of Wilmcote, not far from Stratford. Two daughters were born to them before William's birth—Joan, baptized in 1558, and Margaret, baptized in 1562—but both died in infancy. William was thus their third child, though the eldest of those who survived infancy. After him were born Gilbert (1566), another Joan (1569), Anne (1571), Richard (1574), and Edmund (1580).

Very little is positively known (though much is conjectured) about Shakespeare's boyhood and education. We know that for some years after William's birth his father's rise in Stratford society and municipal affairs continued. Many local offices came to him in rapid succession: ale-taster, burgess (a kind of constable), assessor of fines, chamberlain (town

treasurer), high bailiff (a kind of magistrate). alderma
(town) councilor), and chief alderman in 1571. As the so
of a man of such eminence in Stratford, Shakespeare ur
doubtedly attended the local Grammar School. This he wa
entitled to do free of charge. his father being a town councilor
No records of the school are extant, so that we do not knov
how good a pupil he was nor what subjects he studied. I
is probable that he covered the usual Elizabethan curriculum
an "A B C book," the catechism in Latin and English, Lati
grammar, the translation of Latin authors, and perhaps som
Greek grammar and translation as well. But family circum
stances appear to have curtailed his formal education before i
was complete, for shortly before William reached his four
teenth birthday his father's rising fortunes abruptly passe
their zenith.

Although we do not know all the facts, it is apparent tha
about the year 1578, having gone heavily into debt, Joh
Shakespeare lost two large farms inherited by his wife fron
her father. Thereafter, he was involved in a series of lawsuits
and lost his post on the Stratford town council. Matters go
steadily worse for him, until finally in 1586 he was declare
a bankrupt. But by this time the future poet-dramatist wa
already a family man himself.

In 1582, in the midst of his father's legal and financia
crises—and perhaps because of them—Shakespeare marrie
Anne, daughter of Richard Hathaway (recently deceased)
of the village of Shottery near Stratford. The *Episcopa
Register* for the Diocese of Worcester contains their marriage
record, dated November 28, 1582; he was then in hi
eighteenth year and his wife in her twenty-sixth. On May 2(
of the following year the *Stratford Parish Register* recorde
the baptism of their first child, Susanna; and on February 2
1585, the baptism of a twin son and daughter named Hammet
and Judith.

These facts are all that are known of Shakespeare's early
life. How he supported his family, whether he took up some
trade or profession, how long he continued to live in Stratford
we do not know for certain. Tradition and conjecture have

bestowed on him many interim occupations between his marriage and his appearance in London in the early fifteen-nineties: printer, dyer, traveling-player, butcher, soldier, apothecary, thief—it reads like a children's augury-rhyme (when buttons or cherry-stones are read to learn one's fate). Perhaps only the last-named "pursuit" requires some explanation. According to several accounts, one of them appearing in the first *Life* of Shakespeare by Nicholas Rowe (1709), Shakespeare fell into bad company sometime after his marriage, and on several occasions stole deer from the park of Sir Thomas Lucy, a substantial gentleman of Charlecote, near Stratford. According to Rowe:

> For this he was prosecuted by that gentleman, as he thought somewhat too severely; and in order to revenge that ill-usage, he made a ballad upon him . . . and was obliged to leave his business and family in Warwickshire, for some time, and shelter himself in London.

The story has been repeated in varying forms by most subsequent biographers, but its authenticity is doubted by many who repeat it.

Another much more attractive story, which, however, if true, does not necessarily deny the authenticity of Rowe's, is that Shakespeare during the so-called "lost years" was a schoolmaster. This, indeed, appears to be somewhat better substantiated. John Aubrey, seventeenth-century biographer and antiquary, in his *Brief Lives* (1681) declares that he had learned from a theatrical manager, whose father had known Shakespeare, that the dramatist "had been in his younger years a schoolmaster in the country." This may, then, account, in part at least, for the years between his marriage and his arrival in London about the year 1591. It is interesting to note that in two of his early plays Shakespeare includes a schoolmaster among his characters: Holofernes of *Love's Labour's Lost* and Pinch of *The Comedy of Errors*. But let us hope that neither is intended to be Shakespeare's portrait of himself!

However he may have occupied himself in the interim, we know that by 1592 he was already a budding actor and play-

wright in London. In that year Robert Greene in his auto-
biographical pamphlet *A Groatsworth of Wit*, referring to the
young actors and menders of old plays who were, it seemed
to him, gaining undeserved glory from the labours of their
betters (both by acting their plays and by rewriting them),
wrote as follows:

> Yes trust them not: for there is an upstart Crow, beautified
> with our feathers, that with his Tygers heart wrapt in a
> Players hyde, supposes he is as well able to bombast out
> blanke verse as the best of you: and being an absolute
> *Johannes factotum*, is in his owne conceit the onely Shake-
> scene in a countrey.

"Shakescene" is clearly Shakespeare. The phrase "upstart
Crow" probably refers to his country origins and his lack
of university education. "Beautified with our feathers" probably means that he uses the other playwrights' words for his
own aggrandisement either in plays in which he acts or in
those he writes himself. "Tygers heart wrapt in a Players
hyde" is a parody of a line in III *Henry VI*, one of the
earliest plays ascribed to Shakespeare. And the Latin phrase
Johannes factotum, meaning Jack-of-all-trades, suggests that
he was at this time engaged in all sorts of theatrical jobs:
actor, poet, playwright, and perhaps manager as well.

Greene died shortly after making this scurrilous attack on
the young upstart from Stratford, and so escaped the resent-
ment of those he had insulted. But Henry Chettle, himself
a minor dramatist, who had prepared Greene's manuscript
for the printer, in his *Kind-Harts Dreame* (1592), apologized
to Shakespeare for his share in the offence:

> I am as sory as if the original fault had beene my fault, be-
> cause my selfe have seene his demeanor no lesse civill, than
> he excelent in the qualitie he professes: Besides, divers
> of worship have reported his uprightness of dealing, which
> argues honesty, and his facetious grace in writing, that
> approoves his Art.

Thus, in very indirect manner and because of an attack upon
him by an irascible dying man, we learn that Shakespeare

at this time was in fact held in high regard by "divers of worship," that is, by many of high birth, as an upright, honest young man of pleasant manners and manifest skill as actor, poet, and playwright.

Although Shakespeare by 1593 had written, or written parts of, some five or six plays (I, II, and III *Henry VI, Richard III, The Comedy of Errors,* and perhaps *Titus Andronicus*), it was as a non-dramatic poet that he first appeared in print. *Venus and Adonis* and *The Rape of Lucrece,* long narrative poems, both bearing Shakespeare's name, were published in 1593 and 1594 respectively. But thereafter for the next twenty years he wrote almost nothing but drama. In his early period, 1591 to 1596, in addition to the plays named above he wrote *Love's Labour's Lost, The Taming of the Shrew, Two Gentlemen of Verona, Romeo and Juliet, A Midsummer Night's Dream, Richard II,* and *King John.* Then followed his great middle period, 1596 to 1600, during which he wrote both comedies and history-plays: *The Merchant of Venice,* I and II *Henry IV, The Merry Wives of Windsor, Much Ado about Nothing, Henry V, Julius Caesar, As You Like It,* and *Twelfth Night.* The period of his great tragedies and the so-called "dark comedies" followed (1600-1608): *Hamlet, Troilus and Cressida, All's Well that Ends Well, Measure for Measure, Othello, King Lear, Macbeth, Antony and Cleopatra, Timon of Athens,* and *Coriolanus.* The last phase of his career as dramatist, 1608 to 1613, sometimes called "the period of the romances," produced *Pericles, Prince of Tyre, Cymbeline, The Winter's Tale, The Tempest,* parts of *Henry VIII,* and perhaps parts of *The Two Noble Kinsmen.* Many other plays were ascribed to him, but it is doubtful that he had a hand in any but those we have named. Long before his death in 1616 his name held such magic for the public that merely to print it on the title page of any play assured its popular acclaim. The "upstart Crow" had come a long way since 1592.

He had come a long way too from the economic straits that may well have driven him to London many years before. We know, for example, from the records of tax assessments that by 1596 Shakespeare was already fairly well-to-do. This is further borne out by his purchasing in the following year a substantial house known as New Place and an acre of land in Stratford for £60, a sizable sum in those days. In 1602 he made a further purchase of 107 acres at Stratford for £320, and a cottage and more land behind his estate at New Place. But his life during this time was not quite unclouded. His only son, Hamnet, died in 1596 at the age of eleven years, his father in 1601, and his mother in 1608. All three were buried in Stratford. More happily he saw, in 1607, the marriage of his daughter Susanna to Dr. John Hall, an eminent physician of Stratford, and, in the following year, the baptism of his granddaughter, Elizabeth Hall.

Shakespeare's retirement to Stratford appears to have been gradual, but by 1613, if not earlier, he seems to have settled there, though he still went up to London occasionally. Of the last months of his life we know little. We do know that in February, 1616, his second daughter, Judith, married Thomas Quiney. We know that on March 25, apparently already ill, Shakespeare revised and signed his will, among other bequests leaving to his wife his "second best bed with the furniture." A month later he was dead, dying on his fifty-second birthday, April 23, 1616. He was buried in the chancel of Holy Trinity Church, Stratford, on April 26.

HIS TIMES

Shakespeare lived during the English Renaissance, that age of transition that links the Mediaeval and the Modern world. Inheriting the rich traditions of the Middle Ages in art, learning, religion, and politics, rediscovering the great legacies of classical culture, the men of the Renaissance went on to new and magnificent achievements in every phase of human endeavour. No other period in history saw such varied and prolific development and expansion. And the reign of Elizabeth I (1558-1603), Shakespeare's age, was the High Renaissance in England.

Development and expansion—these are the watchwords of

the age, and they apply to every aspect of life, thought, and activity. The universe grew in immensity as men gradually abandoned the old Ptolemaic view of a finite, earth-centered universe, accepting the enormous intellectual challenge of the illimitable cosmos of Copernicus's theory and Galileo's telescope. The earth enlarged, too, as more of its surface was discovered and charted by explorers following the lead of Columbus, Cabot, Magellan, and Vespucci. England itself expanded as explorers and colonizers, such as Frobisher, Davis, Gilbert, Raleigh, Grenville, Drake, and others, carried the English flag into many distant lands and seas; as English trade and commerce expanded with the opening of new markets and new sources of supply; as English sea power grew to protect the trading routes and fend off rivals, particularly Spain, the defeat of whose Invincible Armada in 1588 greatly advanced English national pride at home, and power and prestige abroad.

The world of ideas changed and expanded, too. The rediscovery and reinterpretation of the classics, with their broad and humane view of life, gave a new direction and impetus to secular education. During the Middle Ages theology had dominated education, but now the language, literature, and philosophy of the ancient world, the practical arts of grammar, logic, and rhetoric, and training in morals, manners, and gymnastics assumed the major roles in both school and university—in other words, an education that fitted one for life in the world here and now replaced one that looked rather to the life hereafter. Not that the spiritual culture of man was neglected. Indeed, it took on a new significance, for as life in this world acquired new meaning and value, religion assumed new functions, and new vitality to perform them, as the bond between the Creator and a new kind of creation.

It was, of course, the old creation—man and nature—but it was undergoing great changes. Some of these we have already seen, but the greatest was in man's conception of himself and his place in nature. The Mediaeval view of man was generally not an exalted one. It saw him as more or

less depraved, fallen from Grace as a result of Adam's sin;
and the things of this world, which was also "fallen," as of
little value in terms of his salvation. Natural life was thought
of mainly as a preparation for man's entry into Eternity. But
Renaissance thought soon began to rehabilitate man, nature,
and the things of this life. Without denying man's need for
Grace and the value of the means of salvation provided by
the Church, men came gradually to accept the idea that
there were "goods", values, "innocent delights" to be had in
the world here and now, and that God had given them for
man to enjoy. Man himself was seen no longer as wholly
vile and depraved, incapable even of desiring goodness, but
rather as Shakespeare saw him in *Hamlet*:

> What a piece of work is man! how noble in reason! how
> infinite in faculty! in form and moving how express and ad-
> mirable! in action how like an angel! in apprehension how
> like a god! the beauty of the world! the paragon of animals!

And this is the conception of man that permeates Elizabethan thought and literature. It does not mean that man
is incorruptible, immune to moral weakness and folly. Shakespeare has his villains, cowards, and fools. But man is none
of these by nature; they are distortions of the true form of
man. Nature framed him for greatness, endowed him with
vast capacities for knowledge, achievement, and delight, and
with aspirations that may take him to the stars. "O brave
new world, That has such people in 't!"

The chief object of man's aspiring mind is now the natural
world, whose "wondrous architecture," says Marlowe's Tam-
burlaine, our souls strive ceaselessly to comprehend, "Still
climbing after knowledge infinite." Hamlet, too, speaks of "this
goodly frame, the earth . . . this brave o'erhanging firmament,
this majestical roof fretted with golden fire." No longer the
ruins of a fallen paradise and the devil's, nature is seen as
man's to possess, her beauty and wonder to be sought after
and enjoyed, her energies to be controlled and used—as
Bacon expressed it, "for the glory of the Creator and the relief
of man's estate."

It was, indeed, a very stirring time to be alive in. New vistas were breaking upon the human mind and imagination everywhere. It was a time like spring, when promise, opportunity, challenge and growth appeared where none had been dreamed of before. Perhaps this is why there is so much poetry of springtime in the age of Shakespeare.

HIS THEATRE

There were many theatres, or playhouses, in Shakespeare's London. The first was built in 1576 by James Burbage and was called the *Theatre*. It was built like an arena, with a movable platform at one end, and had no seats in the pit, but had benches in the galleries that surrounded it. It was built of wood, and cost about £200. Other famous playhouses of Shakespeare's time, for the most part similarly constructed, included the Curtain, the Bull, the Rose, the Swan, the Fortune, and, most famous of them all, the Globe. It was built in 1599 by the sons of James Burbage, and it was here that most of Shakespeare's plays were performed. Since more is known about the Globe than most of the others, I shall use it as the basis of the brief account that follows of the Elizabethan playhouse.

As its name suggests the Globe was a circular structure (the second Globe, built in 1614 after the first burned down, was octagonal), and was open to the sky, somewhat like a modern football or baseball stadium, though much smaller. It had three tiers of galleries surrounding the central "yard" or pit, and a narrow roof over the top gallery. But most interesting from our viewpoint was the stage—or rather *stages* —which was very different from that of most modern theatres. These have the familiar "picture-frame" stage: a raised platform at one end of the auditorium, framed by curtains and footlights, and viewed only from the front like a picture. Shakespeare's stage was very different.

The main stage, or *apron* as it was called, jutted well out into the pit, and did not extend all the way across from side to side. There was an area on either side for patrons to sit

or stand in, so that actors performing on the apron could be
viewed from three sides instead of one. In addition there was
an inner stage, a narrow rectangular recess let into the wall
behind the main stage. When not in use it could be closed
by a curtain drawn across in front; when open it could be
used for interior scenes, arbor scenes, tomb and anteroom
scenes and the like. On either side of this inner stage were
doors through which the main stage was entered. Besides the
inner and outer stages there were no fewer than four other
areas where the action of the play, or parts of it, might be
performed. Immediately above the inner stage, and corre-
sponding to it in size and shape, was another room with its
front exposed. This was the upper stage, and was used for
upstairs scenes, or for storage when not otherwise in use. In
front of this was a narrow railed gallery, which could be used
for balcony scenes, or ones requiring the walls of a castle or
the ramparts of a fortress. On either side of it and on the
same level was a window-stage, so-called because it consisted
of a small balcony enclosed by windows that opened on
hinges. This permitted actors to stand inside and speak from
the open windows to others on the main stage below. In all
it was a very versatile multiple stage and gave the dramatist
and producer much more freedom in staging than most
modern theatres afford. It is interesting to note that some of
the new theatres today have revived certain of the features
of the Elizabethan stage.

Very little in the way of scenery and backdrops was used.
The dramatist's words and the imagination of the audience
supplied the lack of scenery. No special lighting effects were
possible since plays were performed in the daylight that
streamed in through the unroofed top of the three-tiered en-
closure that was the playhouse. Usually a few standard stage-
props were on hand: trestles and boards to form a table,
benches and chairs, flagons, an altar, artificial trees, weapons,
a man's severed head, and a few other items. Costumes were
usually elaborate and gorgeous, though no attempt was
made to reproduce the dress of the time and place portrayed
in the play.

Play production in Shakespeare's time was clearly very different from that of ours, but we need have no doubts about the audience's response to what they saw and heard on stage. They came, they saw, and the dramatist conquered, for they kept coming back for more and more. And despite the opposition that the theatre encountered from Puritans and others, who thought it the instrument of Satan, the theatre in Shakespeare's time flourished as one of the supreme glories of a glorious age.

                        —DAVID G. PITT
                        Memorial University of
                        Newfoundland.

INTRODUCTION TO
Hamlet

A PLAY FOR ALL SEASONS

Hamlet, written at the close of the 16th century, is the first of Shakespeare's "Four Great Tragedies"; *Othello*, *Macbeth* and *King Lear* were yet to come. Each is an undoubted masterpiece, yet it is *Hamlet* which invariably asserts itself as the playwright's most fascinating achievement. For over 350 years it has remained the most popular, the most performed, the most investigated, and the most enigmatic of all of Shakespeare's plays.

Hamlet was first published, in a mangled version, in 1603, at the height of the Renaissance. Even though it derives ultimately from a twelfth century chronicle by the Danish historian Saxo Grammaticus, it is intensely Elizabethan in many aspects. The court of Claudius, King of Denmark, and the court of Elizabeth, Queen of England, are virtually indistinguishable in this play; the actors who come to Elsinore are strongly reminiscent of those from London companies who toured the provinces in Shakespeare's day; Osric, a typical parasite of the aristocracy, is obviously the Elizabethan court fop; and Hamlet himself, the Prince of Denmark, is the epitome of the Renaissance and Humanist "Ideal Man," a "noble mind," and

> The courtier's, soldier's, scholar's, eye, tongue, sword;
> The expectancy and rose of the fair state,
> The glass of fashion and the mould of form,
> The observed of all observers . . .

Yet though the play is thus rooted in its own time, *Hamlet* seems to have a rapport with all ages and all centuries. It speaks as eloquently to the twentieth century as it did to the 17th, 18th, and 19th, and it is not surprising to find that it has been played in "modern" or contemporary dress in *each* of these periods.

The reasons for the play's enduring appeal both in the study and on the stage are not hard to find. *Hamlet* is crowded with visual excitement: a ghost stalking about the ramparts in full armor, court pageantry and intrigue, a play within a play, the marching of soldiers, a brawl in a graveyard, and a duel replete with poisoned rapiers. Its language, though intricate and occasionally foreign to our ears, is a magnificently tempered instrument, always poetic and highly wrought, yet tense, direct, and natural. There is, too, its elements of humor, often bitter and ironic, which sustain rather than dissipate the intensity of the action.

But it is especially the prince himself, Hamlet, who is responsible for the enormous interest of the play. Hamlet is the most "familiar" of all of Shakespeare's tragic heroes; he never loses his dignity or his princeliness; yet he communicates to us in a way which is immediate and elemental. In the presence of Lear or Othello, we are awed, but capable of distancing ourselves from their passions; in the presence of Hamlet, we are immersed in his problems. Confronted by his particular task, to avenge the murder of his father, his questions, his inward agonies, his doubts are an intensification of a pattern familiar to most of us who have lesser, perhaps, but nevertheless personally formidable tasks to perform. Hamlet has erroneously been called Everyman. He is no such abstraction but he is uncomfortably close to the kind of person who has thought at one time or another of the potential disintegration of his love, his life, his world—probably any man. *Hamlet* endures as a play because its hero suffers precisely this.

HAMLET, REVENGE!—THE TRADITION

A fuller understanding of the play and the actions of its central character requires some historical perspective. *Hamlet* belongs to one of the most popular sub-genres of Elizabethan drama—the Revenge Tragedy, or, as a variation and refinement thereof is called, the tragedy of blood. The terms are accurate descriptions of this kind of play: revenge and blood are its hallmarks, and *Hamlet*, whose main motivation is revenge, fits neatly into the category; there are no less than nine deaths in the play, one before it begins and eight during the course of the action.

The revenge tragedy has classical origins in Senecan closet drama, but it burst into popularity in Elizabethan England with the performance of Thomas Kyd's *The Spanish Tragedy* in the late 1580's. This play, the first great English revenge play, initiated a vogue which was to extend far into the 17th century, and it is generally believed that its author was also the writer of a pre-Shakespeare *Hamlet* which is now lost. *The Spanish Tragedy* is important to a study of *Hamlet* for two reasons, not only because it was exceedingly popular in its own day, but because through its influence it set in motion a series of dramatic devices and situations which become "conventional" in the revenge plays which follow it: for example, the use of a supernatural agent who spurs the hero on to his revenge; madness, both real and feigned, on the part of the protagonist; delay in the accomplishment of revenge, either because of doubt on the part of the avenger or because he cannot find a suitable occasion to carry out his task. Finally, it sets aside the normal response to make a moral judgment upon revenge, by treating it as a duty which the hero must undertake.

All of these appear in *Hamlet*, including the device of the "play within a play," which Kyd had formerly used to help his hero obtain blood justice. With just these bare facts in mind, and the realization that the plot of *Hamlet* is little more than a series of incidents eventually leading up to the slaughter of all its principals, including the hero, one would be inclined to call the play nothing more than a "conventional melodrama."

ACTION AND THEMES

But this would be a superficial judgment, though the "story" of *Hamlet* lends credence to this view. At its simplest, the play is about a sensitive young Prince who is informed by the

ghost of his father that he has been murdered by the man
who is now King of Denmark and new husband to Hamlet's
mother. The ghost charges Hamlet to avenge this "foul and
most unnatural murder," a duty which the Prince accepts
without hesitation. The rest of the play is concerned with
Hamlet's process of revenge-taking: he assumes the guise of
madness, ostensibly to forestall suspicion of his true motives,
but though a number of months elapse, and though he often
resolves to take his revenge, he does nothing. Finally, foolishly
participating in a duel in which he is mortally wounded by a
poisoned sword, Hamlet turns upon the king and kills him in
a blind fury.

This bare outline belies the complexity of the play, however. Shakespeare chooses to invest what looks superficially
to be nothing more than a sensational tale with a variety of
interest and a philosophical probing into the nature of life,
death, and man. In doing so, he unleashes a torrent of questions which in the long run are much more profound than the
question of ultimate revenge. This is not to say that Shakespeare does this overtly, or polemically; he does it with a
consummate and unobtrusive artistry by building it into the
warp and woof of his central character, Hamlet.

It has been justly remarked that *Hamlet* is a play written
in the interrogative mood. It does, in fact, begin with a question, Bernardo's fearful "Who's there?" and from this moment
on an unrelenting atmosphere of doubt, distrust, and suspicion pervades the play. Hamlet, plunged into this milieu of
a world at odds with itself and everyone in it, becomes its
chief inquisitor. His questions are fundamental: on Life: "To
be, or not to be?"; on Death: "Dost thou think Alexander
lookt o' this fashion i'th'earth? . . . And smelt so?"; on
Man: "How like a god! . . . And yet, to me, what is this
quintessence of dust?"; and on himself: "What should such
fellows as I do crawling between earth and heaven?" Add
to this the precariousness of Hamlet's situation: is the ghost
a demonic or heaven-sent apparition? Who are his friends?
Whom can he trust? Kill Claudius?—when?

This theme of a quest for certainty in an uncertain world
is intensified by the theme of corruption, disease, and decay

Francisco, for some unexplained reason, is "sick at heart"; Marcellus sets the tone for the whole nation: "Something is rotten in the state of Denmark." Hamlet projects and applies this view to the whole universe: "Fie on't! . . . 'tis an unweeded garden that grows to seed," and later, ". . . this goodly frame, the earth, seems to me a sterile promontory . . . a foul and pestilent congregation of vapours." The language and imagery of the play is charged with this attitude: even Claudius admits he speaks a "painted word" like "the harlot's cheek beautied with plast'ring art."

Thus the world of *Hamlet* is a world of essential dissolution, and a world where one has lost his way. This helps to explain not only the complexity of the play, but also in some measure some of the inconsistencies in the development of the plot and Hamlet's character. It has often been noticed that after the prayer scene (III, iii), Hamlet's actions tend to draw sympathy away from rather than to him. This is true, for the movement of the play in terms of Hamlet's character falls sharply into two parts: at first, we are wholly sympathetic to him; later, when we see Hamlet in the process of hardening his heart, a tension is set up between what he was and what he has become.

What Hamlet does become is akin to classical stoicism. After the graveyard scene in Act V, he reaches a point of resignation which is the only thing that can save him from pitching over the brink of despair he has been teetering on. "If it be not now, yet it will come: the readiness is all," he tells Horatio. To translate this into twentieth century terms, Hamlet has reached an existentialist viewpoint: there is little to be done, and everything to be endured. Hence Hamlet's utter indifference to the duel which eventually precipitates his revenge—and his death.

It is in this fashion that Shakespeare transforms what ordinarily would have been "conventional" and "melodramatic" into something much more. In fact, though *Hamlet* derives from the revenge play tradition, it completely transcends this heritage. It does so because its main character is a far from ordinary man: the task of avenging his murdered father—a simple one as far as Laertes, in a similar position, is concerned

—becomes for Hamlet an excruciating experience which wil
cause him to sound the depths of hell on earth, to question
all existence. Because of this, it is no exaggeration to say tha
in the end he pays a higher price for his ultimate reveng
than his life.

THE "TROUBLE" WITH HAMLET

The "trouble" with Hamlet lies in the involutions of hi
character. He is, as Ophelia's words indicate, a singularly
accomplished young man: courtier, swordsman, and scholar
He is also a connoisseur of drama, an engaging wit, a biting
satirist, and deeply given to philosophical speculation and
inquiry. He has attended Wittenburg, Martin Luther's university, and one of the most volatile on the continent during
the Renaissance. Thus it would seem he is a formidable man
one at the centers of action both physically and intellectually

And yet Hamlet has been habitually condemned as a mar
of inaction, of indecisiveness and procrastination with regard
to the one thing which he resolves early in the play to make
the focus of his life: the avenging of his father's murder. The
question is, when he does have a certainty, "the motive and
the cue for passion," why does he delay in killing Claudius?
It is a question that has occupied critics of Hamlet for many
generations, and it is not one to be easily resolved.

There have been many arguments which lend partia
support to Hamlet's delay. Circumstantial factors, for example
certainly provide impediments. Hamlet does not doubt the
reality of his father's ghost, but he *does* doubt its validity, a
least momentarily. Then, too, how much of his madness is
feigned, how much of it real? On a number of occasions he
appears to be too excited and unhinged, so much so that the
act of revenge is the furthest thing from his mind. Claudius
suspects him, and uses Ophelia, Rosencrantz, and Guildenstern in attempts to trap him, more reasons which cause
Hamlet to tread cautiously.

There are psychological arguments, based primarily on the
temperament of Hamlet. Coleridge calls him "a man living in
meditation," and ascribes his delay to an over-introspective

and speculative nature. Hamlet is thus guilty of "thinking too precisely on th'event," a man who "continually resolves to do, yet does nothing but resolve." A. C. Bradley finds reasons for Hamlet's delay in his undoubtedly melancholic and brooding tendencies. This bent is intensified in the beginning of the play: Hamlet is deeply affected by his mother's "o'erhasty marriage" to Claudius, and revolted by the fact that she is now, technically, engaged in an incestuous relationship; also, his father's death has plunged him into inconsolable grief, and the girl he loves is suddenly not only denied to him but used as a decoy to ensnare him. All these conspire to make him even more melancholy, a condition which eventually paralyzes his will and reduces him to mere fatalism. Goethe attacks the problem by placing Hamlet's delay in a moral perspective: the Prince is sensitive and idealistic; he shrinks from taking his vengeance because it is a task morally repugnant to his sensitive nature.

More recently, A. J. A. Waldock has argued that the delay in *Hamlet* is more apparent than real. He points out that in fact there are only three occasions in the play when delay is *dramatically* a question: Hamlet's soliloquies at II, ii, pp. 74-76 and IV, iv, pp. 132-33, and the second visitation of his father's ghost. In the study, the question of delay is an issue; on the stage, it is buried by the seeping, hurried flow of the action.

Some of these arguments are more cogent than others, but all of them have in common a tendency to explain the play in terms of Hamlet, rather than Hamlet in terms of the play—in other words, taking parts for the whole. To focus on delay as the salient characteristic of the Prince is to ignore the complexity of Hamlet and the world in which he lives. Treating Hamlet with too narrow a perspective has been an employment that many ciritics have made love to, and not a few of them have been hoist with their own petard in the process.

The twentieth century has attempted to widen the range and approach to Hamlet's character, so much so that a distinctly anti-Hamlet school has developed, a phenomenon that would have amazed critics one hundred years ago. G. Wilson Knight, for example, calls Hamlet "the ambassador of death," arguing that his intense preoccupation with images of disease and corruption, his disgust at the world, his morbid brooding on death, all point to a mind essentially unhealthy. Hamlet's callous treatment of Ophelia, his brutal rationalization for not killing Claudius at his prayers, his insensitive reaction to his butchering of Polonius, his indifference to the deaths of Rosencrantz and Guildenstern, and his obsession to berate his mother for her sensuality in marrying Claudius, in spite of the ghost's exhortation to "leave her to heaven," all provide a picture very different from the conception of a noble prince set upon by the slings and arrows of outrageous fortune.

This, too, is a one-sided interpretation, but it is a reaction which points to the necessity of examining Hamlet in relation to the characters who surround him and in terms of the values he espouses. It also forces us to align our predisposition to sympathize with Hamlet, and to realize that Shakespeare has put him in a number of situations in which it is impossible not to make moral and comparative judgments of the Prince.

THE OTHER CHARACTERS

The point is, simply, that *Hamlet* is not a "one-man play," a conception that has been unfortunately encouraged by the star system in the theatre and literary critics turned psychoanalysts in the library. The play suffers in both cases if Hamlet remains in splendid isolation.

Claudius especially, in himself and not just in his relationship to Hamlet, is crucial to any interpretation of the play. He is certainly the "villain" of the piece, but he is definitely no stereotype villain. Seen through Hamlet's eyes, he is a murderer, lecher, drunkard, smiling hypocrite, and a crafty politician who "Popt in" between the election and Hamlet's hopes. Seen in himself, as King of Denmark, who has been chosen with the approbation of the lords of the realm, he emerges in a different perspective.

Claudius is in fact every inch a king, and obviously capable of ruling well. He deals with the Fortinbras problem early in the play with competence and dispatch. Moreover, when Laertes assaults his castle and bursts upon Claudius with hot demands for blood, Claudius coolly outfaces him and turns a potentially disastrous situation to his own advantage. It is true also that Claudius, as the play shows him, does really love Gertrude, and is solicitous for her welfare. There is no textual evidence to support the view that he is the lecher Hamlet paints him to be.

But the most disturbing thing about Claudius is that he is a villain who shows remorse, and one whom Shakespeare audaciously allows to show that remorse to the disadvantage of his hero. Hamlet's decision *not* to kill Claudius while the latter kneels in prayer, because he wants the king's "heels to kick at heaven," is in shocking contradiction to Horatio's "Good night, sweet prince" at the end of the play. It is not necessary to rehabilitate Claudius, however, but it is important to see that Shakespeare has made him a worthy antagonist of Hamlet, and in the process emphasized the frailty of his hero.

Laertes and Fortinbras function similarly with regard to Hamlet. They are both impetuous and hotheaded young men, given to prompt and decisive action. Their positions in the play exactly parallel that of Hamlet: both have lost fathers whom they feel duty-bound to avenge in their own fashions. As such, they stand in marked contrast to Hamlet, who has the same obligation, but not nearly the same kind of direct vitality in carrying it out. By the images of their causes, Hamlet sees the portraiture of his, and there is no doubt that Shakespeare uses them to intensify Hamlet's dilemma and to emphasize his inability to take revenge.

Polonius is perhaps one of the more unattractive characters in the play; he is on the verge of senility, garrulous and over-impressed with his own rhetoric. He is a tyrant to his daughter and a man who spies upon his own son. But he serves a number of important dramatic functions. Shakespeare uses him first of all as a butt for Hamlet and a source of comedy: it is by means of Polonius' ineptitude and pretentiousness that much of Hamlet's wit and irony is given full scope. He also precipitates the action through his beloved intrigues, and, indirectly, because of Hamlet's callous reaction to his death, contributes to a more just estimation of the

Prince's character. Rosencrantz and Guildenstern, virtually indistinguishable in their roles, serve similar functions.

The two women in the play, Gertrude and Ophelia, have a number of characteristics in common. Both are weak-willed and are essentially victims of the action, rather than participants in it. Ophelia is apparently in love with Hamlet, yet she is willing to repulse him at her father's command, as well as engage in a plot designed to show the true nature of his madness. In many ways she is a fragile creature, more pathetic than admirable, and one whose harsh fate seems incommensurate with her misdeeds.

Horatio, technically, is a dramatic mechanism. He functions primarily as friend and confidant to Hamlet, one who provides information necessary to move the play along, and one left to pick up the pieces at the end. But, limited though his role is, Shakespeare has made much of him thematically.

Horatio emerges as an oasis of values in a play which seems at times completely void of certainty. Hamlet pinpoints him accurately when he describes him as "one, in suff'ring all, that suffers nothing." Horatio is no court flatterer; he is always controlled and thoughtful, never "passion's slave." An honest man then, and a stoic by nature. As such he is everything that Hamlet admires and would like to be. But most important, his terse and stern reaction to Hamlet's treatment of Rosencrantz and Guildenstern, his equilibrium in the face of Hamlet's probings into death, his good advice to his friend not to duel with Laertes, all serve to establish him as a pole of cool reason and stability, in stark contrast to Hamlet. Horatio does not speak often in this play, but when he does, he speaks with the authority of one who is always in the right.

—GINO J. MATTEO
Department of English
St. Michael's College
University of Toronto

STUDY QUESTIONS

ACT ONE

1. A good exposition serves to launch a play by: capturing the interest of the audience, introducing characters, establishing the lines of conflict, and contributing to the dominant atmosphere of the play. How well does Act One serve these functions, and in what ways?

2. What is the significance of Bernardo being first to challenge Francisco rather than vice versa? What tone does this establish?

3. In the first scene, how does setting, atmosphere, dialogue, and character contribute to suspense?

4. Discuss the character of Claudius as it appears in Scene two. How does Hamlet's reaction to him modify and influence our judgment?

5. Consider Hamlet's soliloquy, I, ii, pp. 16-17, on these counts: (1) character revelation, (2) Hamlet's state of mind, (3) his attitude toward his mother, (4) its technique of comparison, and (5) imagery.

6. Contrast the attitudes of Hamlet and Horatio towards the ghost. How do their reactions reveal differences between the two men?

7. What is the significance of Hamlet's writing on his tablets after the ghost has charged him to take revenge?

8. What evidence is there in Scene V which indicates that Hamlet's madness will be feigned? What evidence is there that it is real? What is the true situation?

ACT TWO

1. What developments have occurred since the end of Act One and how are they revealed?

2. Write a brief character sketch of Polonius as he is revealed in this Act. Consider his attitude toward his own family, the king, and Hamlet, and his language as indicators.

3. What evidence is there to support the view that Hamlet really does love Ophelia and has gone mad because she refuses his love?

4. "Rosencrantz and Guildenstern are type characters, mere pawns to advance the plot." Support or refute this view by citing evidence from the text.

5. Discuss Shakespeare's use of irony in the exchanges between Hamlet and Polonius. What new facets of Hamlet's character are revealed?

6. What dramatic function does the arrival of the players at Elsinore serve? Consider its appropriateness to the action of the plot and revelation of character.

7. Does the story of Hecuba have any relation to the rest of the act, or is it merely an interlude?

8. What are the chief purposes and techniques of a soliloquy? What specific purposes are served by Hamlet's soliloquy at the end of Act II?

9. Write a brief essay summarizing all the impediments, both external and internal, which have been placed in the way of Hamlet's revenge.

ACT THREE

1. How does Hamlet's soliloquy, "To be, or not to be," confirm or clarify traits in his character which have already been revealed? What themes in the play are strengthened by this speech?

2. If you were staging *Hamlet*, how would you contrive to make Hamlet aware that he is being spied upon during his interview with Ophelia?

3. In your opinion, why does Hamlet fail to act after "the mousetrap" assures him of the guilt of Claudius? What does this indicate about his (a) madness, and (b) attitude toward revenge?

4. Analyze the logic of Claudius' speech, "O, my offence is rank!" Does it indicate repentance or remorse on his part? Depending on your answer, how does this affect the interpretation of Hamlet's decision not to kill him at this point?

5. "The Closet scene is crucial to an interpretation of Hamlet's character in the latter part of the play." Discuss the

scene in relation to: Hamlet's attitude toward his mother, his ability to kill Polonius and his attitude towards it, and the significance of the second visitation of the ghost.

ACT FOUR

1. How do the different reactions of Hamlet and Claudius to the death of Polonius provide measurements of their characters?

2. Shakespeare uses humor in the scene in which Claudius interviews Hamlet about Polonius. Why is humor used at this point, and how does it differ from earlier humorous episodes in the play?

3. What is the dramatic significance of Hamlet's meeting with the captain of Fortinbras' army?

4. Contrast the behaviour of Laertes and Hamlet in terms of how they react to the deaths of their fathers.

5. Write a brief essay on Shakespeare's treatment of madness as it is seen in Hamlet and Ophelia.

6. Nemesis is the principle of retributive justice, whereby all receive their just deserts. Does this principle operate with regard to the deaths of Polonius and Ophelia?

7. Our sympathy toward Hamlet has been shaken in Acts III and IV. How does Shakespeare regain that sympathy by the end of Act IV?

ACT FIVE

1. Is the Graveyard scene appropriate to the atmosphere and movement of the play? Explain in detail its contributions to the main themes of *Hamlet*.

2. Contrast the attitudes of Hamlet and Horatio with regard to Hamlet's consideration of life and death in the Graveyard Scene.

3. What are Hamlet's reasons for brawling with Laertes in the grave of Ophelia? Estimate their sincerity in their demonstrations of grief.

4. How does the principle of retributive justice apply to Hamlet's handling of Rosencrantz and Guildenstern? What is Horatio's reaction?

5. Discuss the use of language as a source of irony in Hamlet's interview with Osric.

6. The denouement, or falling action, is the final unraveling of the play. What evidence is there in this act to suggest that Hamlet has willingly foregone control of the action? Has his character changed significantly by this point?

7. Horatio is left at the end of the play to tell "of accidental judgements, casual slaughters." Does the action of the whole play and its catastrophe provide enough evidence to suggest that his words are correct? Discuss.

8. Why is it appropriate that Fortinbras should become successor to the throne of Denmark?

General Questions

1. Discuss the theories explaining Hamlet's delay (see Introduction), refuting or supporting them by reference to the text.

2. Assume you are a director of *Hamlet*: what interpretations would you use and how would you make them clear in the following situations: (1) Hamlet's confrontation with Claudius in Act I, Scene 2. (2) Hamlet's meeting with Ophelia while Claudius and Polonius look on unobserved. (3) The Prayer scene. (4) The Closet scene. (5) The Graveyard scene.

3. Indicate how Shakespeare uses the supernatural in terms of atmosphere, suspense, plot development, and character revelation.

4. Discuss the device of contrast and its effectiveness as it is used between: Act I, scene 1, and Act I, scene 2; Hamlet and the First Player; Hamlet and Polonius.

5. The crisis of a play is its chief turning point in the complication of the action. What do you consider to be the turning point of *Hamlet*, and what are your reasons?

6. Trace (a) the images of corruption and (b) the images of acting and illusion in *Hamlet*, indicating what they contribute to the development of themes and characters in the play.

7. Identify the following passages, indicating speaker and occasion, and commenting on: style, significance to plot or character, and thematic relevance:

(a)   But, to the quick o'th' ulcer:—
   Hamlet comes back: what would you undertake,
   To show yourself your father's son in deed
   More than in words?

(b) Not a whit, we defy augury; there's a special prov-

idence in the fall of a sparrow. If it be now, 'tis not
to come; if it be not to come, it will be now; if it be
not now, yet it will come: the readiness is all.

(c)   And now remains
That we find out the cause of this effect—
Or rather say, the cause of this defect,
For this effect defective comes by cause;
Thus it remains, and the remainder thus.

(d)   Now, whether it be
Bestial oblivion, or some craven scruple
Of thinking too precisely on th'event,—
A thought, which, quarter'd, hath but one part wis-
    dom
And ever three parts coward,—I do not know
Why yet I live to say 'This thing's to do.'

(e)   Give me that man
That is not passion's slave, and I will wear him
In my heart's core, ay, in my heart of heart.

HAMLET
A PRINCE OF DENMARK

DRAMATIS PERSONAE

CLAUDIUS, *King of Denmark.*
HAMLET, *son to the late, and nephew to the present king.*
POLONIUS, *lord chamberlain.*
HORATIO, *friend to Hamlet.*
LAERTES, *son to Polonius.*
VOLTIMAND,
CORNELIUS,
ROSENCRANTZ, } *courtiers.*
GUILDENSTERN,
OSRIC,
A GENTLEMAN,
A PRIEST.
MARCELLUS, } *officers.*
BERNARDO,
FRANCISCO, *a soldier.*
REYNALDO, *servant to Polonius.*
PLAYERS.
TWO CLOWNS, *grave-diggers.*
FORTINBRAS, *Prince of Norway.*
A CAPTAIN.
ENGLISH AMBASSADORS.
GERTRUDE, *Queen of Denmark, and mother to Hamlet.*
OPHELIA, *daughter to Polonius.*
LORDS, LADIES, OFFICERS, SOLDIERS, SAILORS, MESSENGERS, *and
other* ATTENDANTS.
GHOST *of Hamlet's father.*

SCENE—*Denmark.*

Hamlet

ACT I

ACT I

On the battlements of Elsinore castle in Denmark, Horatio, told of a ghostly apparition resembling the late King Hamlet, joins Marcellus and Bernardo on watch. The ghost appears again, and the three men resolve to tell Prince Hamlet what has occurred. Hamlet is seen for the first time at a formal gathering of the court. His uncle, Claudius, now King of Denmark and newly married to Hamlet's mother, Gertrude, sends emissaries to the King of Norway whose young nephew Fortinbras is threatening war against Denmark, and gives permission to Laertes, son of his counsellor Polonius, to return to France. Claudius and Gertrude are rebuffed in their attempts to console Hamlet. Left alone, he speaks of his disillusionment with the world and his revulsion at his mother's marriage to Claudius. Informed by Horatio of the apparition, he decides to join the watch. Laertes departs, and Polonius, suspicious of Hamlet's intentions toward his daughter, tells Ophelia she must not see him. A few nights later Hamlet meets his father's ghost, which tells him he has been murdered by Claudius, and urges vengeance. Hamlet vows to seek it, and will feign madness to avoid suspicion.

ACT I. Scene I.

Elsinore. A platform before the castle.

Francisco *at his post. Enter to him* Bernardo.

BERNARDO. — officer

Who's there?

FRANCISCO. — soldier

Nay, answer me: stand, and unfold yourself.[1]

BERNARDO.

Long live the king!

FRANCISCO.

Bernardo?

BERNARDO.

He.

FRANCISCO.

You come most carefully upon your hour.[2]

BERNARDO.

'Tis now struck twelve; get thee to bed, Francisco.

---

[1] unfold yourself: identify yourself.
[2] You come most carefully upon your hour: you are right on time.

FRANCISCO.

For this relief much thanks: 'tis bitter cold,
And I am sick at heart.

BERNARDO.

Have you had quiet guard?

FRANCISCO.

                    Not a mouse stirring.

BERNARDO.

Well, good night.
If you do meet Horatio and Marcellus,
The rivals[1] of my watch, bid them make haste.

FRANCISCO.

I think I hear them.—Stand, ho! Who is there?

        Enter HORATIO *and* MARCELLUS.

HORATIO.

Friends to this ground.

MARCELLUS.

               And liegemen to the Dane.[2]

FRANCISCO.

Give you good night.

MARCELLUS.

            O, farewell, honest soldier:
Who hath relieved you?

FRANCISCO.

           Bernardo has my place.
Give you good night.   [*Exit*

MARCELLUS.

        Holla! Bernardo!

BERNARDO.

                  Say,—
What, is Horatio there?

---

[1] rivals: fellow guards.
[2] the Dane: King of Denmark.

HORATIO.

A piece of him.[1]

BERNARDO.

Welcome, Horatio:—welcome, good Marcellus.

MARCELLUS.

What, has this thing[2] appear'd again to-night?

BERNARDO.

I have seen nothing.

MARCELLUS.

Horatio says 'tis but our fantasy,
And will not let belief take hold of him
Touching this dreaded sight, twice seen of us:
Therefore I have entreated him along
With us to watch the minutes of this night;[3]
That, if again this apparition come,
He may approve our eyes,[4] and speak to it.

HORATIO.

Tush, tush, 'twill not appear.

BERNARDO.

Sit down awhile;
And let us once again assail your ears,
That are so fortified against our story,
What we two nights have seen.

HORATIO.

Well, sit we down,
And let us hear Bernardo speak of this.

BERNARDO.

Last night of all,
When yond same star that's westward from the pole[5]

---

[1] A piece of him: he is not wholeheartedly there.
[2] this thing: a reference to the ghost of Hamlet's father.
[3] to watch the minutes of this night: to stand watch.
[4] approve our eyes: believe as we do.
[5] pole: the North Pole.

Had made his course t'illume that part of heaven
Where now it burns, Marcellus and myself,
The bell then beating[1] one,—

MARCELLUS.
Peaee, break thee off; look, where it comes again!

Enter GHOST.

BERNARDO.
In the same figure, like the king that's dead.

MARCELLUS.
Thou art a scholar; speak to it, Horatio.

BERNARDO.
Looks it not like the king? mark it, Horatio.

HORATIO.
Most like:—it harrows[2] me with fear and wonder.

BERNARDO.
It would be spoke to.

MARCELLUS.
Question it, Horatio.

HORATIO.
What art thou, that usurp'st this time of night,
Together with that fair and warlike form
In which the majesty of buried Denmark[3]
Did sometimes march? by heaven I charge thee, speak!

MARCELLUS.
It is offended.

BERNARDO.
See, it stalks away!

HORATIO.
Stay! speak, speak! I charge[4] thee, speak!

[*Exit* GHOST.

MARCELLUS.
'Tis gone, and will not answer.

---

[1] **beating:** striking.
[2] **harrows:** disturbs.
[3] **buried Denmark:** the dead king.
[4] **charge:** command.

BERNARDO.

How now, Horatio! you tremble, and look pale:
Is not this something more than fantasy?
What think you on't?

HORATIO.

Before my God, I might not this believe
Without the sensible and true avouch[1]
Of mine own eyes.

MARCELLUS.

Is it not like the king?

HORATIO.

As thou art to thyself:
Such was the very armour he had on
When he th'ambitious Norway[2] combated;
So frown'd he once, when, in an angry parle,[3]
He smote the sledded Polacks[4] on the ice.
'Tis strange.

MARCELLUS.

Thus twice before, and jump[5] at this dead hour,
With martial stalk hath he gone by our watch.

HORATIO.

In what particular thought to work I know not;
But, in the gross and scope of my opinion,
This bodes some strange eruption to our state.

MARCELLUS.

Good now, sit down, and tell me, he that knows,
Why this same strict and most observant watch
So nightly toils the subject of the land;[6]
And why such daily cast of brazen cannon,
And foreign mart[7] for implements of war;
Why such impress[8] of shipwrights, whose sore task
Does not divide the Sunday from the week;[9]
What might be toward, that this sweaty haste

---

[1] avouch: proof. [2] Norway: ruler of Norway. [3] parle: parley. [4] Polacks: Polish soldiers. [5] jump: exactly. [6] toils the subject of the land: excites the citizens. [7] foreign mart: foreign trade. [8] impress: draft. [9] Does not divide the Sunday from the week: that is they work seven days a week.

Doth make the night joint-labourer with the day:[1]
Who is't that can inform me?

HORATIO.

That can I;
At least, the whisper goes so. Our last king,
Whose image even but now appear'd to us,
Was, as you know, by Fortinbras of Norway,
Thereto prickt on by a most emulate pride,[2]
Dared to the combat; in which our valiant Hamlet—
For so this side of our known world esteem'd him—
Did slay this Fortinbras; who, by a seal'd compact,[3]
Well ratified by law and heraldry,[4]
Did forfeit, with his life, all those his lands
Which he stood seized of to the conqueror:
Against the which, a moiety competent[5]
Was gaged [6] by our king; which had return'd
To the inheritance of Fortinbras,
Had he been vanquisher; as, by the same cov'nant,
And carriage of the article design'd,[7]
His fell to Hamlet. Now, sir, young Fortinbras,
Of unimproved mettle hot and full,
Hath in the skirts of Norway, here and there,
Sharkt up a list[8] of lawless resolutes,
For food and diet,[9] to some enterprise
That hath a stomach in't: which is no other—
As it doth well appear unto our state—
But to recover of us, by strong hand
And terms compulsative,[10] those foresaid lands
So by his father lost: and this, I take it,
Is the main motive of our preparations,
The source of this our watch, and the chief head

---

[1] Doth make the night joint-labourer with the day: that is, they labor day and night. [2] emulate pride: jealous pride. [3] sealed compact: agreed-upon terms. [4] by law and heraldry: heraldic law; laws that govern combat. [5] a moiety competent: an adequate share. [6] gaged: pledged. [7] carriage of the article design'd: the point of the agreement. [8] sharkt up a list: snatched up desperadoes. [9] food and diet: meat for the grinder (war). [10] compulsative: compulsory.

Of this post-haste and romage[1] in the land.

BERNARDO.

I think it be no other but e'en so:
Well may it sort[2] that this portentous figure
Comes armed through our watch; so like the king
That was and is the question[3] of these wars.

HORATIO.

A mote it is to trouble the mind's eye.
In the most high and palmy[4] state of Rome,
A little ere the mightiest Julius fell,
The graves stood tenantless, and the sheeted dead
Did squeak and gibber in the Roman streets:
As, stars with trains of fire[5] and dews of blood,
Disasters in the sun; and the moist star,
Upon whose influence Neptune's empire stands,[6]
Was sick almost to doomsday with eclipse:
And even the like precurse[7] of the fierce events—
As harbingers[8] preceding still the fates,[9]
And prologue to the omen coming on[10]—
Have heaven and earth together demonstrated
Unto our climatures and countrymen.—
But, soft, behold! lo, where it comes again!

Enter GHOST *again.*

I'll cross it, though it blast me.—Stay, illusion!
If thou hast any sound, or use of voice,
Speak to me:
If there be any good thing to be done,
That may to thee do ease, and grace to me,
Speak to me:
If thou art privy to thy country's fate,
Which, happily, foreknowing may avoid,
O, speak!
Or if thou hast uphoarded in thy life

---

[1] **romage**: stir; commotion. [2] **well may it sort**: it may well be. [3] **question**: object. [4] **palmy**: mighty; victorious. [5] **stars with trains of fire**: comets. [6] **the moist star/Upon whose influence Neptune's empire stands**: the moon (a lunar eclipse); **Neptune**: god of the sea. [7] **precurse**: precursor; forerunner. [8] **harbingers**: heralds. [9] **the fates**: the Fates of Destiny; Clotho, Lachesis, and Atropos. [10] **omen coming on**: approaching calamity.

Extorted treasure in the womb of earth,
For which, they say, you spirits oft walk in death,

                           [*Cock crows.*

Speak of it:—stay, and speak!—Stop it, Marcellus.

    MARCELLUS.

Shall I strike at it with my partisan?[1]

    HORATIO.

Do, if it will not stand.

    BERNARDO.

                   'Tis here!

    HORATIO.

                          'Tis here!

    MARCELLUS.

'Tis gone!   [*Exit* GHOST.

We do it wrong, being so majestical,
To offer it the show of violence;
For it is, as the air, invulnerable,
And our vain blows malicious mockery.[2]

    BERNARDO.

It was about to speak when the cock crew.

    HORATIO.

And then it started like a guilty thing
Upon a fearful summons. I have heard,
The cock, that is the trumpet to the morn,
Doth with his lofty and shrill-sounding throat
Awake the god of day; and at his warning,
Whether in sea or fire, in earth or air,
Th'extravagant[3] and erring spirit hies
To his confine: and of the truth herein
This present object made probation.[4]

    MARCELLUS.

It faded on the crowing of the cock.

---

[1] partisan: a pike; a halberd; a weapon resembling a long-handled ax.
[2] malicious mockery: petty annoyance.
[3] extravagant: wandering.
[4] made probation: gave proof.

Some say, that ever 'gainst that season comes
Wherein our Saviour's birth is celebrated,
The bird of dawning singeth all night long:
And then, they say, no spirit dare stir abroad;
The nights are wholesome; then no planets strike,[1]
No fairy takes,[2] nor witch hath power to charm;
So hallow'd and so gracious is the time.

HORATIO.

So have I heard, and do in part believe it.
But, look, the morn, in russet mantle[3] clad,
Walks o'er the dew of yon high eastern hill:
Break we our watch up: and, by my advice,
Let us impart what we have seen to-night
Unto young Hamlet; for, upon my life,
This spirit, dumb to us, will speak to him:
Do you consent we shall acquaint him with it,
As needful in our loves, fitting our duty?[4]

MARCELLUS.

Let's do't, I pray; and I this morning know
Where we shall find him most convenient.

[Exeunt.

SCENE II

A room of state in the castle.

Enter the KING, QUEEN, HAMLET, POLONIUS, LAERTES,
VOLTIMAND, CORNELIUS, LORDS, and ATTENDANTS.

KING.

Though yet of Hamlet our dear brother's death
The memory be green;[5] and that it us befitted
To bear our hearts in grief, and our whole kingdom

---

[1] planets strike: affect with misfortune.
[2] takes: beguiles.
[3] russet mantle: reddish-brown cloth.
[4] needful in our loves, fitting our duty: do our duty as friends.
[5] green: fresh.

To be contracted in one brow of woe;
Yet so far hath discretion fought with nature,
That we with wisest sorrow think on him,
Together with remembrance of ourselves.
Therefore our sometime sister, now our queen,
Th'imperial jointress[1] of this warlike state,
Have we, as 'twere with a defeated [2] joy,—
With one auspicious, and one dropping eye,[3]
With mirth in funeral, and with dirge in marriage,
In equal scale weighing delight and dole,[4]—
Taken to wife: nor have we herein barr'd
Your better wisdoms, which have freely gone
With this affair along:—for all, our thanks.
Now follows, that you know, young Fortinbras,
Holding a weak supposal [5] of our worth,
Or thinking by our late dear brother's death
Our state to be disjoint and out of frame,[6]
Colleagued with the dream of his advantage,[7]—
He hath not fail'd to pester us with message,
Importing the surrender of those lands
Lost by his father, with all bands of law,
To our most valiant brother. So much for him.—
Now for ourself, and for this time of meeting:
Thus much the business is:—we have here writ
To Norway, uncle of young Fortinbras,—
Who, impotent and bed-rid, scarcely hears
Of this his nephew's purpose,—to suppress
His further gait herein,[8] in that the levies,
The lists, and full proportions, are all made
Out of his subject:—and we here dispatch
You, good Cornelius, and you, Voltimand,
For bearers of this greeting to old Norway;
Giving to you no further personal power

---

[1] jointress: a widow who shares an inheritance. [2] defeated: over
come. [3] With one auspicious, and one dropping eye: i.e., glad and
sad at the same time. [4] dole: grief. [5] weak supposal: poor opinion.
[6] disjoint and out of frame: state of utter confusion. [7] Colleagued
with the dream of his advantage: coupled with his dream of
superiority. [8] His further gait herein: his war preparations.

To business with the king, more than the scope
Of these delated [1] articles allow.
Farewell; and let your haste commend your duty. [2]

    CORNELIUS *and* VOLTIMAND.

In that and all things will we show our duty.

    KING.

We doubt it nothing: heartily farewell.

                      [*Exeunt* VOLTIMAND *and* CORNELIUS.

And now, Laertes, what's the news with you?
You told us of some suit; what is't, Laertes?
You cannot speak of reason to the Dane,
And lose your voice: what would'st thou beg, Laertes,
That shall not be my offer, not thy asking?
The head is not more native [3] to the heart,
The hand more instrumental to the mouth,
Than is the throne of Denmark to thy father.
What wouldst thou have, Laertes?

    LAERTES.

                     My dread lord,
Your leave [4] and favour to return to France;
From whence though willingly I came to Denmark,
To show my duty in your coronation;
Yet now, I must confess, that duty done,
My thoughts and wishes bend again toward France,
And bow them to your gracious leave and pardon.

    KING.

Have you your father's leave? What says Polonius?

    POLONIUS.

He hath, my lord, wrung from me my slow leave
By laboursome petition; and, at last,

---

[1] delated: tendered.
[2] let your haste commend your duty: let haste show your devotion to duty.
[3] native: related.
[4] leave: permission to leave.
[5] laboursome petition: repeated pleas.

Upon his will I seal'd my hard consent:[1]
I do beseech you, give him leave to go.

    KING.

Take thy fair hour,[2] Laertes; time be thine,
And thy best graces spend it at thy will!—
But now, my cousin[3] Hamlet, and my son,—

    HAMLET [aside].

A little more than kin, and less than kind.

    KING.

How is it that the clouds still hang on you?[4]

    HAMLET.

Not so, my lord; I am too much i'th'sun.

    QUEEN.

Good Hamlet, cast thy nighted colour[5] off,
And let thine eye look like a friend on Denmark.
Do not for ever with thy vailed lids
Seek for thy noble father in the dust:
Thou know'st 'tis common,—all that live must die,
Passing through nature to eternity.

    HAMLET.

Ay, madam, it is common.

    QUEEN.

                    If it be,
Why seems it so particular with thee?

    HAMLET.

Seems, madam! nay, it is; I know not 'seems.'
'Tis not alone my inky cloak, good mother,
Nor customary suits of solemn black,
Nor windy suspiration of forced breath,[6]
No, nor the fruitful river in the eye,[7]
Nor the dejected haviour[8] of the visage,
Together with all forms, moods, shows of grief,

---

[1] seal'd my hard consent: unbreakable promise. [2] Take thy fair hour: enjoy your youth. [3] cousin: used by Shakespeare in addressing another person of similar rank. [4] How is it that the clouds still hang on you?: why are you still sad? [5] knighted colour: dark mourning clothes. [6] windy suspiration of forced breath: insincere sighs. [7] fruitful river in the eye: copious weeping. [8] havior: behavior.

That can denote me truly: these, indeed, seem,
For they are actions that a man might play:
But I have that within which passeth show;
These but the trappings and the suits of woe.

    KING.

'Tis sweet and commendable in your nature, Hamlet,
To give these mourning duties to your father:
But, you must know, your father lost a father;
That father lost, lost his; and the survivor bound,
In filial obligation, for some term
To do obsequious sorrow: but to persever
In obstinate condolement,[1] is a course
Of impious stubbornness, 'tis unmanly grief:
It shows a will most incorrect to heaven,[2]
A heart unfortified, a mind impatient;
An understanding simple and unschool'd:
For what we know must be, and is as common
As any the most vulgar[3] thing to sense,
Why should we, in our peevish opposition,
Take it to heart? Fie! 'tis a fault to heaven,
A fault against the dead, a fault to nature,
To reason most absurd; whose common theme
Is death of fathers, and who still hath cried,
From the first corse[4] till he that died to-day,
'This must be so.' We pray you, throw to earth
This unprevailing[5] woe; and think of us
As of a father: for let the world take note,
You are the most immediate to our throne;[6]
And with no less nobility of love
Than that which dearest father bears his son,
Do I impart toward you. For your intent
In going back to school in Wittenberg,

---

[1] obstinate condolement: long-lasting sorrow.
[2] incorrect to heaven: not in accordance with divine will.
[3] vulgar: common; familiar.
[4] corse: corpse.
[5] unprevailing: serving no good end.
[6] immediate to our throne: closest in succession.

It is most retrograde[1] to our desire:
And we beseech you, bend you[2] to remain
Here, in the cheer and comfort of our eye,
Our chiefest courtier, cousin, and our son.

QUEEN.

Let not thy mother lose her prayers, Hamlet:
I pray thee, stay with us; go not to Wittenberg.

HAMLET.

I shall in all my best obey you, madam.

KING.

Why, 'tis a loving and a fair reply:
Be as ourself in Denmark.[3]—Madam, come;
This gentle and unforced accord of Hamlet
Sits smiling to my heart: in grace whereof,[4]
No jocund health that Denmark drinks to-day,
But the great cannon to the clouds shall tell;
And the king's rouse[5] the heaven shall bruit[6] again,
Re-speaking[7] earthly thunder. Come away.

[Exeunt all but HAMLET

HAMLET.

O, that this too too solid flesh would melt,
Thaw, and resolve itself into a dew!
Or that the Everlasting had not fixt
His canon 'gainst self-slaughter! O God! God!
How weary, stale, flat, and unprofitable
Seem to me all the uses of this world!
Fie on't! O, fie! 'tis an unweeded garden,
That grows to seed; things rank and gross in nature
Possess it merely. That it should come to this!
But two months dead!—nay, not so much, not two:
So excellent a king; that was, to this,

---

[1] **retrograde:** contrary; opposed. [2] **bend you:** to submit to our
wishes. [3] **Be as ourself in Denmark:** enjoy the same prerogative
as the king and queen. [4] **in grace whereof:** in honor of. [5] **rouse:**
drinking; toasting; carousings. [6] **bruit:** report; echo. [7] **Re-speaking:**
repeating.

Hyperion[1] to a satyr:[2] so loving to my mother,
That he might not beteem[3] the winds of heaven
Visit her face too roughly. Heaven and earth!
Must I remember? why, she would hang on him,
As if increase of appetite had grown
By what it fed on: and yet, within a month,—
Let me not think on't,—Frailty, thy name is woman!—
A little month; or e'er those shoes were old
With which she follow'd my poor father's body,
Like Niobe,[4] all tears;—why she, even she—
O God! a beast, that wants discourse of reason,[5]
Would have mourn'd longer—married with my uncle,
My father's brother; but no more like my father
Than I to Hercules:[6] within a month;
Ere yet the salt of most unrighteous tears
Had left the flushing[7] in her galled [7] eyes,
She married:—O, most wicked speed, to post
With such dexterity to incestuous sheets!
It is not nor it cannot come to good:
But break, my heart,—for I must hold my tongue!

Enter HORATIO, MARCELLUS, *and* BERNARDO.

HORATIO.

Hail to your lordship!

HAMLET.

      I am glad to see you well:
Horatio,—or I do forget myself.

HORATIO.

The same, my lord, and your poor servant ever.

HAMLET.

Sir, my good friend; I'll change that name with you:[8]

---

[1] Hyperion: the sun god; also symbol of manly beauty. [2] satyr:
ancient Greek deities, often represented as having the attributes of
a horse or goat, and having a fondness for revelry. [3] beteem:
allow. [4] Niobe: the proud Queen of Thebes, in Greek mythology,
punished by the goddess Leto through the death of her children.
[5] wants discourse of reason: lacks the ability to reason. [6] Hercules:
mythological hero noted for his great physical strength. [7] flushing:
red; inflamed; galled: irritated. [8] I'll change that name with you:
that is, let us call each other "friend."

And what make you from Wittenberg,[1] Horatio?—Marcellus?

MARCELLUS.

My good lord,—

HAMLET.

I am very glad to see you.—Good even, sir.—
But what, in faith, make you from Wittenberg?

HORATIO.

A truant disposition, good my lord.

HAMLET.

I would not hear your enemy say so;
Nor shall you do mine ear that violence
To make it truster of your own report
Against yourself: I know you are no truant.
But what is your affair in Elsinore?
We'll teach you to drink deep ere you depart.

HORATIO.

My lord, I came to see your father's funeral.

HAMLET.

I pray thee, do not mock me, fellow-student;
I think it was to see my mother's wedding.

HORATIO.

Indeed, my lord, it follow'd hard upon.[2]

HAMLET.

Thrift, thrift, Horatio! the funeral baked meats
Did coldly furnish[3] forth the marriage tables.
Would I had met my dearest foe[4] in heaven
Or ever I had seen that day, Horatio!—
My father,—methinks I see my father.

HORATIO.

O, where, my lord?

HAMLET.

                    In my mind's eye, Horatio.

---

[1] what make you from Wittenburg?: what are you doing (away) from Wittenberg?
[2] hard upon: close upon.
[3] coldly furnish: served as leftovers.
[4] dearest foe: worst enemy.

HORATIO.

I saw him once; he was a goodly king.

HAMLET.

He was a man, take him for all in all,
I shall not look upon his like again.

HORATIO.

My lord, I think I saw him yesternight.

HAMLET.

Saw? who?

HORATIO.

My lord, the king your father.

HAMLET.

      The king my father!

HORATIO.

Season your admiration[1] for a while
With an attent[2] ear; till I may deliver,
Upon the witness of these gentlemen,
This marvel to you.

HAMLET.

     For God's love, let me hear.

HORATIO.

Two nights together had these gentlemen,
Marcellus and Bernardo, on their watch,
In the dead vast and middle of the night,
Been thus encounter'd. A figure like your father,
Armed at point,[3] exactly, cap-a-pe.[3]
Appears before them, and with solemn march
Goes slowly and stately by them: thrice he walkt
By their opprest[4] and fear-surprised eyes,
Within his truncheon's[5] length; whilst they, distill'd [6]
Almost to jelly with the act of fear,
Stand dumb, and speak not to him. This to me

---

[1] **Season your admiration:** temper your wonder.
[2] **attent:** attentive.
[3] **at point:** completely; **cap-a-pe:** from head to toe.
[4] **opprest:** incredulous.
[5] **truncheon:** staff (symbol of authority).
[6] **distill'd:** reduced.

In dreadful secrecy impart they did;
And I with them the third night kept the watch:
Where, as they had deliver'd, both in time,
Form of the thing, each word made true and good,
The apparition comes: I knew your father;
These hands are not more like.[1]

HAMLET.
                                    But where was this?

MARCELLUS.
My lord, upon the platform where we watcht.

HAMLET.
Did you not speak to it?

HORATIO.
                            My lord, I did;
But answer made it none: yet once methought
It lifted up its head, and did address
Itself to motion, like as it would speak:
But even then the morning cock crew loud;
And at the sound it shrunk in haste away,
And vanisht from our sight.

HAMLET.
                            'Tis very strange.

HORATIO.
As I do live, my honour'd lord, 'tis true;
And we did think it writ down in our duty
To let you know of it.

HAMLET.
Indeed, indeed, sirs, but this troubles me.
Hold you the watch to-night?

MARCELLUS AND BERNARDO.
                            We do, my lord.

HAMLET.
Arm'd, say you?

---

[1] **These hands are not more like:** Horatio means that the gho
resembled Hamlet's father as closely as Horatio's hands resembl
each other.

MARCELLUS AND BERNARDO.

Arm'd, my lord.

HAMLET.

From top to toe?

MARCELLUS AND BERNARDO.

My lord, from head to foot.

HAMLET.

Then saw you not his face?

HORATIO.

O, yes, my lord; he wore his beaver[1] up.

HAMLET.

What, lookt he frowningly?

HORATIO.

A countenance more in sorrow than in anger.

HAMLET.

Pale or red?

HORATIO.

Nay, very pale.

HAMLET.

And fixt his eyes upon you?

HORATIO.

Most constantly.

HAMLET.

I would I had been there.

HORATIO.

It would have much amazed you.

HAMLET.

Very like,[2] very like. Stay'd it long?

HORATIO.

While one with moderate haste might tell[3] a hundred.

MARCELLUS AND BERNARDO.

Longer, longer.

---

[1] beaver: the lower part of a helmet (visor).
[2] very like: very likely.
[3] tell: count.

HORATIO.

Not when I saw't.

HAMLET.

His beard was grizzled,[1]—no?

HORATIO.

It was, as I have seen it in his life,
A sable silver'd.

HAMLET.

I will watch to-night;
Perchance 'twill walk again.

HORATIO.

I warrant it will.

HAMLET.

If it assume my noble father's person,
I'll speak to it, though hell itself should gape,[2]
And bid me hold my peace. I pray you all,
If you have hitherto conceal'd this sight,
Let it be tenable[3] in your silence still;
And whatsoever else shall hap[4] to-night,
Give it an understanding, but no tongue:[5]
I will requite[6] your loves. So, fare you well:
Upon the platform, 'twixt eleven and twelve,
I'll visit you.

ALL.

Our duty to your honour.

HAMLET.

Your loves, as mine to you: farewell.

[*Exeunt all but* HAMLET.

My father's spirit in arms! all is not well;
I doubt[7] some foul play: would the night were come!
Till then sit still, my soul: foul deeds will rise,

---

[1] **grizzled:** mixed with gray. [2] **gape:** open. [3] **tenable:** held. [4] **hap:** happen. [5] **Give it an understanding, but no tongue:** recognize it but say nothing. [6] **requite:** return. [7] **doubt:** suspect.

Though all the earth o'erwhelm them, to men's eyes. [*Exit.*

SCENE III.

A room in POLONIUS' *house.*

Enter LAERTES *and* OPHELIA.

LAERTES.

My necessaries are embarkt: farewell:
And, sister, as the winds give benefit,
And convoy is assistant,[1] do not sleep,
But let me hear from you.

OPHELIA.

     Do you doubt that?

LAERTES.

For Hamlet, and the trifling of his favour,[2]
Hold it a fashion, and a toy in blood.[3]
A violet in the youth of primy nature,[4]
Forward,[5] not permanent, sweet, not lasting,
The perfume and suppliance[6] of a minute;
No more.

OPHELIA.

  No more but so?[7]

LAERTES.

     Think it no more:
For nature, crescent,[8] does not grow alone
In thews[9] and bulk; but, as this temple waxes,[10]
The inward service of the mind and soul
Grows wide withal. Perhaps he loves you now;
And now no soil nor cautel[11] doth besmirch
The virtue of his will: but you must fear,
His greatness weigh'd,[12] his will is not his own;
For he himself is subject to his birth:
He may not, as unvalued persons do,

---

[1] as the winds give benefit,/And convoy is assistant: at every favorable opportunity and when the means of conveyance are available. [2] the trifling of his favour: his little attentions. [3] a fashion, and a toy in blood: a thing of the moment, and a fleeting passion. [4] the youth of primy nature: in the bud of youth. [5] forward: spirited. [6] suppliance: need. [7] No more but so?: is that all? [8] crescent: developing. [9] thews: strength. [10] temple waxes: body grows. [11] cautel: trickery. [12] weigh'd: considered.

Carve for himself;[1] for on his choice depends
The safety and health of this whole state;
And therefore must his choice be circumscribed
Unto the voice and yielding of that body,[2]
Whereof he is the head. Then if he says he loves you,
It fits your wisdom so far to believe it,
As he in his particular act and place
May give his saying deed;[3] which is no further
Than the main voice of Denmark goes withal.[4]
Then weigh what loss your honour may sustain,
If with too credent[5] ear you list his songs;
Or lose your heart; or your chaste treasure open
To his unmaster'd importunity.
Fear it, Ophelia, fear it, my dear sister;
And keep you in the rear of your affection,[6]
Out of the shot and danger of desire.
The chariest[7] maid is prodigal enough,
If she unmask her beauty to the moon:
Virtue itself scapes not calumnious strokes:
The canker galls the infants of the spring,[8]
Too oft before their buttons[9] be disclosed;
And in the morn and liquid dew of youth
Contagious blastments are most imminent.
Be wary, then; best safety lies in fear:
Youth to itself rebels, though none else near.

       OPHELIA.

I shall th'effect of this good lesson keep,
As watchman to my heart. But, good my brother,
Do not, as some ungracious[10] pastors do,
Show me the steep and thorny way to heaven;
Whilst, like a puft and reckless libertine,
Himself the primrose path of dalliance treads,

---

[1] **Carve for himself**: be guided by his wishes alone. [2] **that body**: the state. [3] **give his saying deed**: suit the words to action. [4] **withal**: at the same time. [5] **credent**: gullible; credulous. [6] **keep you in the rear of your affection**: hold it in check. [7] **chariest**: most diffident [8] **infants of the spring**: early spring buds. [9] **buttons**: buds. [10] **ungracious**: ungodly.

And recks[1] not his own rede.[2]
>
> LAERTES.
>
>   O, fear me not.
> I stay too long:—but here my father comes.

Enter POLONIUS.

A double blessing is a double grace;
Occasion smiles upon a second leave.[3]

POLONIUS.

Yet here, Laertes! aboard, aboard, for shame!
The wind sits in the shoulder of your sail,
And you are stay'd [4] for. There,—my blessing with thee!

                    [*Laying his hand on* LAERTES' *head.*

And these few precepts in thy memory
See thou character. Give thy thoughts no tongue,
Nor any unproportion'd[5] thought his act.
Be thou familiar, but by no means vulgar.[6]
The friends thou hast, and their adoption tried,
Grapple them to thy soul with hoops of steel;[7]
But do not dull thy palm with entertainment
Of each new-hatcht, unfledged comrade. Beware
Of entrance to a quarrel; but being in,
Bear't, that th'opposed may beware of thee.
Give every man thine ear, but few thy voice:
Take each man's censure,[8] but reserve thy judgement.
Costly thy habit as thy purse can buy,
But not exprest in fancy; rich, not gaudy:
For the apparel oft proclaims the man;
And they in France of the best rank and station
Are most select and generous, chief in that.
Neither a borrower nor a lender be:
For loan oft loses both itself and friend;
And borrowing dulls the edge of husbandry.[9]

---

[1] recks: heeds. [2] rede: advice. [3] occasion smiles upon a second leave: the pleasure of a second farewell. [4] stay'd: waited. [5] unproportion'd: unseemly. [6] vulgar: common. [7] Grapple them to thy soul with hoops of steel: hold fast to them. [8] censure: judgment. [9] husbandry: thrift.

This above all,—to thine own self be true;
And it must follow, as the night the day,
Thou canst not then be false to any man.
Farewell: my blessing season this in thee!

LAERTES.

Most humbly do I take my leave, my lord.

POLONIUS.

The time invites you; go, your servants tend.

LAERTES.

Farewell, Ophelia; and remember well
What I have said to you.

OPHELIA.

                 'Tis in my memory lockt,
And you yourself shall keep the key of it.

LAERTES.

Farewell.   [*Exit.*

POLONIUS.

What is't, Ophelia, he hath said to you?

OPHELIA.

So please you, something touching the Lord Hamlet.

POLONIUS.

Marry,[1] well bethought:
'Tis told me, he hath very oft of late
Given private time to you; and you yourself
Have of your audience been most free and bounteous:
If it be so,—as so 'tis put on me,[2]
And that in way of caution,—I must tell you,
You do not understand yourself so clearly
As it behoves my daughter and your honour.
What is between you? give me up the truth.

---

[1] **Marry:** "by the Virgin Mary" (an oath).
[2] **as so 'tis put on me:** as so I am given to understand.

OPHELIA.

He hath, my lord, of late made many tenders[1]
Of his affection to me.

POLONIUS.

Affection! pooh! you speak like a green girl,
Unsifted [2] in such perilous circumstance.
Do you believe his tenders, as you call them?

OPHELIA.

I do not know, my lord, what I should think.

POLONIUS.

Marry, I'll teach you: think yourself a baby;
That you have ta'en these tenders for true pay,[3]
Which are not sterling. Tender yourself more dearly;[4]
Or—not to crack the wind of the poor phrase,[5]
Running it thus—you'll tender me a fool.

OPHELIA.

My lord, he hath importuned me with love
In honourable fashion.

POLONIUS.

Ay, fashion you may call't; go to, go to.

OPHELIA.

And hath given countenance to his speech, my lord,
With almost all the holy vows of heaven.

POLONIUS.

Ay, springes[6] to catch woodcocks. I do know,
When the blood burns, how prodigal the soul
Lends the tongue vows: these blazes, daughter,
Giving more light than heat,—extinct in both,
Even in their promise, as it is a-making,—
You must not take for fire. From this time
Be somewhat scanter of your maiden presence;
Set your entreatments at a higher rate

---

[1] tenders: proffers. [2] unsifted: inexperienced. [3] true pay: real worth.
[4] Tender yourself more dearly: don't offer your favors so easily or
freely. [5] Or—not to crack the wind of the poor phrase: not to
belabor the phrase. [6] springes: snares to catch foolish birds.

Than a command to parley.[1] For Lord Hamlet,
Believe so much in him, that he is young;
And with a larger tether[2] may he walk
Than may be given you: in few,[3] Ophelia,
Do not believe his vows; for they are brokers,[4]—
Not of that dye which their investments show,[5]
But mere implorators of unholy suits,
Breathing[6] like sanctified and pious bawds,[7]
The better to beguile. This is for all,—
I would not, in plain terms, from this time forth,
Have you so slander[8] any moment leisure
As to give words or talk with the Lord Hamlet.
Look to't, I charge you: come your ways.

    OPHELIA.
I shall obey, my lord.   [*Exeunt.*

SCENE IV.

The platform before the castle.
  Enter HAMLET, HORATIO, *and* MARCELLUS.

    HAMLET.
The air bites shrewdly;[9] it is very cold.

    HORATIO.
It is a nipping and an eager air.

    HAMLET.
What hour now?

    HORATIO.
          I think it lacks of twelve.

    MARCELLUS.
No, it is struck.

    HORATIO.
Indeed? I heard it not: then it draws near the season

---

[1] Set your entreatments at a higher rate/Than a command to parley: do not make yourself accessible because of a simple request for a meeting. [2] larger tether: more freedom. [3] in few: in a few words. [4] brokers: procurers (go-betweens). [5] Not of that dye which their investments show: they are not what they seem. [6] breathing: speaking. [7] bawds: panderers. [8] slander: abuse. [9] shrewdly: piercingly.

Wherein the spirit held his wont to walk.[1]

> [*A flourish of trumpets, and ordnance shot off, within.*

What does this mean, my lord?

HAMLET.

The king doth wake to-night, and takes his rouse,[2]
Keeps wassail,[3] and the swaggering up-spring reels;[4]
And, as he drains his draughts of Rhenish[5] down,
The kettle-drum and trumpet thus bray out
The triumph of his pledge.[6]

HORATIO.
                              Is it a custom?

HAMLET.

Ay, marry, is't:
But to my mind,—though I am native here,
And to the manner born,—it is a custom
More honour'd in the breach[7] than the observance.
This heavy-headed revel east and west
Makes us traduced and taxt[8] of other nations:
They clepe[9] us drunkards, and with swinish phrase
Soil our addition;[10] and, indeed, it takes[11]
From our achievements, though perform'd at height,
The pith and marrow of our attribute.[12]
So, oft it chances in particular men,
That, for some vicious mole[13] of nature in them,
As, in their birth,—wherein they are not guilty,
Since nature cannot choose his origin,—
By the o'ergrowth of some complexion,[14]
Oft breaking down the pales and forts of reason;[15]

---

[1] held his wont to walk: was in the habit of walking. [2] rouse:
reveals. [3] Keeps wassail: holds a drinking party. [4] up-spring reels:
spirited dance. [5] Rhenish: Rhine wine. [6] pledge: toast. [7] breach:
neglect. [8] traduced and taxt: belittled and censured. [9] clepe: call.
[10] addition: title. [11] takes: detracts. [12] The pith and marrow of our
attribute: the essence of our quality. [13] vicious mole: imperfection.
[14] complexion: temperament: [15] pales and forts of reason: limits of
reason.

Or by some habit, that too much o'er-leavens[1]
The form of plausive[2] manners;—that these men,—
Carrying, I say, the stamp of one defect,
Being nature's livery,[3] or fortune's star,[4]—
Their virtues else—be they as pure as grace,
As infinite as man may undergo—
Shall in the general censure take corruption
From that particular fault: the dram of eale[5]
Doth all the noble substance of a doubt
To his own scandal.[6]

    HORATIO.

              Look, my lord, it comes!
               Enter GHOST.

    HAMLET.

Angels and ministers of grace defend us!—
Be thou a spirit of health or goblin damn'd,
Bring with thee airs from heaven or blasts from hell,
Be thy intents wicked or charitable,
Thou comest in such a questionable shape,
That I will speak to thee: I'll call thee Hamlet,
King, father, royal Dane: O, answer me!
Let me not burst in ignorance; but tell
Why thy canonized bones, hearsed in death,
Have burst their cerements;[7] why the sepulchre,
Wherein we saw thee quietly inurn'd,
Hath oped his ponderous and marble jaws
To cast thee up again! What may this mean,
That thou, dead corse,[8] again, in complete steel,[9]
Revisit'st thus the glimpses of the moon,
Making night hideous; and we fools of nature
So horridly to shake our disposition
With thoughts beyond the reaches of our souls?

---

[1] o'er-leavens: changes. [2] plausive: agreeable. [3] nature's livery:
nature's endowment. [4] fortune's star: fate's endowment. [5] eale:
evil. [6] scandal: disgrace. [7] cerements: burial shroud. [8] corse: corpse.
[9] complete steel: fully armed.

Say, why is this? wherefore? what should we do?

> [GHOST *beckons* HAMLET.

HORATIO.
It beckons you to go away with it,
As if it some impartment[1] did desire
To you alone.

MARCELLUS.
        Look, with what courteous action
It waves you to a more removed [2] ground:
But do not go with it.

HORATIO.
           No, by no means.

HAMLET.
It will not speak; then I will follow it.

HORATIO.
Do not, my lord.

HAMLET.
        Why, what should be the fear?
I do not set my life at a pin's fee;
And for my soul, what can it do to that,
Being a thing immortal as itself?
It waves me forth again;—I'll follow it.

HORATIO.
What if it tempt you toward the flood,[3] my lord,
Or to the dreadful summit of the cliff
That beetles o'er his base into the sea,
And there assume some other horrible form,
Which might deprive your sovereignty of reason,
And draw you into madness? think of it:
The very place puts toys of desperation,[4]
Without more motive, into every brain,
That looks so many fathoms to the sea,
And hears it roar beneath.

---

[1] impartment: information.
[2] more removed: farther away.
[3] flood: the sea.
[4] toys of desperation: horrible fancies.

HAMLET.

                 It waves[1] me still.—
Go on; I'll follow thee.

MARCELLUS.

You shall not go, my lord.

HAMLET.

              Hold off your hands.

HORATIO.

Be ruled; you shall not go.

HAMLET.

              My fate cries out,
And makes each petty artery in this body
As hardy as the Nemean lion's[2] nerve.—
Still am I call'd:—unhand me, gentlemen;—
By heaven, I'll make a ghost of him that lets[3] me:—
I say, away!—Go on; I'll follow thee.

                   [*Exeunt* GHOST *and* HAMLET.

HORATIO.

He waxes[4] desperate with imagination.

MARCELLUS.

Let's follow; 'tis not fit thus to obey him.

HORATIO.

Have after.[5]—To what issue will this come?

MARCELLUS.

Something is rotten in the state of Denmark.

HORATIO.

Heaven will direct it.

MARCELLUS.

             Nay, let's follow him.

                               [*Exeunt.*

---

[1] waves: beckons.
[2] the Nemean lion: a feared and powerful lion killed by Hercules as the first in the "Twelve Labours of Hercules."
[3] lets: delays; hinders.
[4] waxes: grows.
[5] have after: we'll follow him.

Scene V.

Another part of the platform.
Enter GHOST *and* HAMLET.

HAMLET.
Where wilt thou lead me? speak; I'll go no further.

GHOST.
Mark me.[1]

HAMLET.
        I will.

GHOST.
            My hour is almost come,
When I to sulphurous and tormenting flames
Must render up myself.

HAMLET.
            Alas, poor ghost!

GHOST.
Pity me not, but lend thy serious hearing
To what I shall unfold.

HAMLET.
            Speak; I am bound[2] to hear.

GHOST.
So art thou to revenge, when thou shalt hear.

HAMLET.
What?

GHOST.
I am thy father's spirit;
Doom'd for a certain term to walk the night,
And for the day confined to fast in fires,[3]
Till the foul crimes done in my days of nature
Are burnt and purged away. But that I am forbid
To tell the secrets of my prison-house,

---

[1] Mark me: pay attention to me.
[2] bound: pledged.
[3] Doom'd for a certain term to walk the night,/And for the day confined to fast in fires: he is in Purgatory.

I could a tale unfold, whose lightest word
Would harrow up thy soul; freeze thy young blood;
Make thy two eyes, like stars, start from their spheres;
Thy knotted and combined locks to part,
And each particular hair to stand an end,
Like quills upon the fretful porpentine:[1]
But this eternal blazon[2] must not be
To ears of flesh and blood.—List, list, O, list!—
If thou didst ever thy dear father love,—

HAMLET.

O God!

GHOST.

Revenge his foul and most unnatural murder.

HAMLET.

Murder!

GHOST.

Murder most foul, as in the best it is;
But this most foul, strange, and unnatural.

HAMLET.

Haste me to know't, that I, with wings as swift
As meditation or the thoughts of love,
May sweep to my revenge.

GHOST.

                I find thee apt;
And duller shouldst thou be than the fat weed
That roots itself in ease on Lethe[3] wharf,
Wouldst thou not stir in this. Now, Hamlet, hear:
'Tis given out that, sleeping in my orchard,
A serpent stung me; so the whole ear of Denmark
Is by a forged process[4] of my death
Rankly abused:[5] but know, thou noble youth,

---

[1] porpentine: porcupine.
[2] blazon: message from eternity.
[3] Lethe: the river of Death in mythology.
[4] forged process: false circumstance.
[5] rankly abused: completely deceived.

The serpent that did sting thy father's life
Now wears his crown.   *Claudius*

    HAMLET.

            O my prophetic soul!

My uncle!

    GHOST.

Ay, that incestuous, that adulterate beast,
With witchcraft of his wit, with traitorous gifts,—
O wicked wit and gifts, that have the power
So to seduce!—won to his shameful lust
The will of my most seeming-virtuous queen:
O Hamlet, what a falling-off was there!
From me, whose love was of that dignity,
That it went hand in hand even with the vow
 made to her in marriage; and to decline
Upon a wretch, whose natural gifts were poor
To those of mine!
But virtue, as it never will be moved,
Though lewdness court it in a shape of heaven;
So lust, though to a radiant angel linkt,
Will sate itself in a celestial bed,
And prey on garbage.
But, soft![1] methinks I scent the morning air;
Brief let me be.—Sleeping within my orchard,
My custom always in the afternoon,
Upon my secure hour[2] thy uncle stole,
With juice of cursed hebenon[3] in a vial,
And in the porches of mine ears did pour
The leperous distilment; whose effect
Holds such an enmity with blood of man,
That, swift as quicksilver, it courses through
The natural gates and alleys of the body;
And, with a sudden vigour, it doth posset[4]

---

soft: gently.
Upon my secure hour: while he was off guard.
hebenon: henbane, a poisonous plant.
posset: curdle.

And curd, like eager droppings into milk,
The thin and wholesome blood: so did it mine;
And a most instant tetter barkt about,[1]
Most lazar-like,[2] with vile and loathsome crust
All my smooth body.
Thus was I, sleeping, by a brother's hand
Of life, of crown, of queen, at once dispatcht:[3]
Cut off even in the blossoms of my sin,
Unhousell'd,[4] disappointed, unaneled;[4]
No reckoning made, but sent to my account
With all my imperfections on my head:
O, horrible! O, horrible! most horrible!
If thou hast nature[5] in thee, bear it not;
Let not the royal bed of Denmark be
A couch for luxury and damned incest.
But, howsoever thou pursuest this act,
Taint not thy mind, nor let thy soul contrive
Against thy mother aught: leave her to heaven,
And to those thorns that in her bosom lodge
To prick and sting her. Fare thee well at once!
The glow-worm shows the matin[6] to be near,
And 'gins[7] to pale his uneffectual fire:
Adieu, adieu, adieu! remember me.   [*Exit*

HAMLET.

O all you host of heaven! O earth! what else?
And shall I couple[8] hell?—O, fie!—Hold, hold, my heart;
And you, my sinews, grow not instant old,
But bear me stiffly up.—Remember thee!
Ay, thou poor ghost, while memory holds a seat
In this distracted globe.[9] Remember thee!
Yea, from the table[10] of my memory

---

[1] **instant tetter barkt about**: covered with ulcers. [2] **lazar-like**: leperous. [3] **at once dispacht**: done away with. [4] **Unhousell'd . . . unaneled**: without receiving the sacrament of extreme unction. [5] **nature** humanity. [6] **matin**: morn. [7] **'gins**: begins. [8] **couple**: include. [9] **this distracted globe**: his head. [10] **table**: tablet.

I'll wipe away all trivial fond records,
All saws[1] of books, all forms, all pressures[2] past,
That youth and observation copied there;
And thy commandment all alone shall live
Within the book and volume of my brain,
Unmixt with baser matter: yes, by heaven!—
O most pernicious woman!
O villain, villain, smiling, damned villain!
My tables,—meet it is I set it down,
That one may smile, and smile, and be a villain;
At least I'm sure it may be so in Denmark: [*Writing.*
So, uncle, there you are. Now to my word;
It is, 'Adieu, adieu! remember me:'
I have sworn't.

    HORATIO [*within*].
My lord, my lord,—
        MARCELLUS [*within*].
                Lord Hamlet,—
        HORATIO [*within*].
                        Heaven secure[3] him!
    HAMLET.
So be it!
        HORATIO [*within*].
Illo, ho, ho, my lord!
    HAMLET.
Hillo, ho, ho, boy![4] come, bird, come.
            Enter HORATIO *and* MARCELLUS.
    MARCELLUS.
How is't, my noble lord?
        HORATIO.
                What news, my lord?

---

[1] saws: moral sayings.
[2] pressures: impressions.
[3] secure: protect.
[4] Hillo, ho, ho, boy!: the call of a falconer to his bird.

HAMLET.

O, wonderful!

HORATIO.

Good my lord, tell it.

HAMLET.

                No; you will reveal it.

HORATIO.

Not I, my lord, by heaven.

MARCELLUS.

                Nor I, my lord.

HAMLET.

How say you, then; would heart of man once think it?—
But you'll be secret?

HORATIO *and* **MARCELLUS.**

                Ay by heaven, my lord.

HAMLET.

There's ne'er a villain dwelling in all Denmark
But he's an arrant[1] knave.

HORATIO.

There needs no ghost, my lord, come from the grave
To tell us this.

HAMLET.

                Why, right; you are i'th'right;
And so, without more circumstance at all,[2]
I hold it fit that we shake hands and part:
You, as your business and desire shall point you,—
For every man hath business and desire,
Such as it is;—and for mine own poor part,
Look you, I'll go pray.

HORATIO.

These are but wild and whirling[3] words, my lord.

---

[1] arrant: confirmed.

[2] without more circumstance at all: without more ado.

[3] whirling: confused.

HAMLET.
I'm sorry they offend you, heartily;
Yes, faith, heartily.

HORATIO.
                    There's no offence, my lord.

HAMLET.
Yes, by Saint Patrick, but there is, Horatio,
And much offence too. Touching this vision here,—
It is an honest ghost, that let me tell you:
For your desire to know what is between us,
O'ermaster't as you may.[1] And now, good friends,
As you are friends, scholars, and soldiers,
Give me one poor request.

HORATIO.
What is't, my lord? we will.

HAMLET.
Never make known what you have seen to-night.

HORATIO *and* MARCELLUS.
My lord, we will not.

HAMLET.
                    Nay, but swear't.

HORATIO.
                              In faith,
My lord, not I.

MARCELLUS.
                    Nor I, my lord, in faith.

HAMLET.
Upon my sword.

MARCELLUS.
                    We have sworn, my lord, already.

HAMLET.
Indeed, upon my sword, indeed.

---

[1] O'ermaster't as you may: control your curiosity as you may.

GHOST [*cries under the stage*].

Swear.

HAMLET.

Ah, ha, boy! say'st thou so? art thou there, truepenny?[1]—
Come on,—you hear this fellow in the cellarage,[2]—
Consent to swear.

HORATIO.

Propose the oath, my lord.

HAMLET.

Never to speak of this that you have seen,
Swear by my sword.

GHOST [*beneath*].

Swear.

HAMLET.

Hic et ubique?[3] then we'll shift our ground.—
Come hither, gentlemen,
And lay your hands again upon my sword:
Never to speak of this that you have heard,
Swear by my sword.

GHOST [*beneath*].

Swear.

HAMLET.

Well said, old mole! canst work i'th'earth so fast?
A worthy pioneer![4]—Once more remove, good friends.

HORATIO.

O day and night, but this is wondrous strange!

HAMLET.

And therefore as a stranger give it welcome.
There are more things in heaven and earth, Horatio,
Than are dreamt of in your philosophy.
But come;—

---

[1] truepenny: an honest or trustworthy person.
[2] cellarage: cellar.
[3] *Hic et ubique?*: i.e., here and everywhere.
[4] pioneer: a digger who went ahead of an army and felled trees,
etc., to clear the way for the march.

Here, as before, never, so help you mercy,
How strange or odd soe'er I bear myself,—
As I, perchance, hereafter shall think meet
To put an antic disposition on,[1]—
That you, at such times seeing me, never shall,
With arms encumber'd thus, or this head-shake,
Or by pronouncing of some doubtful phrase,
As 'Well, well, we know,' or 'We could, an if we would,'
Or 'If we list[2] to speak,' or 'There be, an if they might,'
Or such ambiguous giving out, to note
That you know aught of me:—this not to do,
So grace and mercy at your most need help you,
Swear.

GHOST [beneath].

Swear.

HAMLET.

Rest, rest, perturbed spirit!—So, gentlemen,
With all my love I do commend me to you:
And what so poor a man as Hamlet is
May do t'express his love and friending to you,
God willing, shall not lack. Let us go in together;
And still your fingers on your lips, I pray.
The time is out of joint:[3]—O cursed spite,
That ever I was born to set it right!—
Nay, come, let's go together.   [Exeunt.

---

[1] To put an antic disposition on: to play the fool.
[2] list: please.
[3] The time is out of joint: these are bad times.

Hamlet

ACT 2

ACT II

POLONIUS, who has sent an attendant to France to spy on Laertes, is told of Hamlet's deranged behavior toward Ophelia. Deciding that unrequited love has driven Hamlet mad, he hurries off to report this to Claudius. The king, also worried about the cause of Hamlet's "antic disposition," has summoned two friends of Hamlet, Rosencrantz and Guildenstern, and ordered them to observe him closely. After the ambassadors to Norway report a successful mission, Polonius presses his theory of unrequited love, and convinces Claudius to hide with him and observe a meeting between Hamlet and Ophelia. Rosencrantz and Guildenstern are welcomed by Hamlet, who immediately senses their true purpose in visiting him. At the same time, a company of players arrive, and Hamlet, hoping to assure himself of the guilt of Claudius, arranges for them to perform *The Murder of Gonzago*, which he will alter to fit more nearly the circumstances of his father's death. At the end of the act, he berates himself because his vengeance is still not taken, but, unsure of the ghost, resolves to use the play to confirm its story.

ACT II. Scene I.

Elsinore. A room in POLONIUS' *house.*

Enter POLONIUS *and* REYNALDO.

POLONIUS.
Give him this money and these notes, Reynaldo.
REYNALDO.
I will, my lord.
POLONIUS.
You shall do marvellous wisely, good Reynaldo,
Before you visit him, to make inquiry
Of his behaviour.
REYNALDO.
           My lord, I did intend it.
POLONIUS.
Marry, well said; very well said. Look you, sir,
Inquire me first what Danskers[1] are in Paris;
And how, and who, what means, and where they keep,
What company, at what expense; and finding,
By this encompassment and drift of question,[2]
That they do know my son, come you more nearer

---

[1] **Danskers:** Danes.
[2] **encompassment and drift of questions:** roundabout questioning.

Than your particular demands will touch it:[1]
Take you, as 'twere, some distant knowledge of him;
As thus, 'I know his father and his friends,
And in part him;'—do you mark this, Reynaldo?

REYNALDO.

Ay, very well, my lord.

POLONIUS.

'And in part him;—but,' you may say, 'not well:
But, if't be he I mean, he's very wild;
Addicted so and so;'—and there put on him[2]
What forgeries you please; marry, none so rank[3]
As may dishonour him; take heed of that;
But, sir, such wanton,[4] wild, and usual slips
As are companions noted and most known
To youth and liberty.

REYNALDO.

As gaming, my lord.

POLONIUS.

Ay, or drinking, fencing, swearing,
Quarrelling, drabbing.[5]—you may go so far.

REYNALDO.

My lord, that would dishonour him.

POLONIUS.

Faith, no; as you may season it in the charge.[6]
You must not put another scandal on him,
That he is open to[7] incontinency;
That's not my meaning: but breathe his faults so quaintly,[8]
That they may seem the taints[9] of liberty;
The flash and outbreak of a fiery mind;
A savageness in unreclaimed[10] blood,
Of general assault.

---

[1] Than your particular demands will touch it: than your direct questions will produce. [2] put on him: foist on him. [3] rank: coarse; lowly. [4] wanton: unrestrained. [5] Drabbing: carousing with loose women. [6] season it in the charge: weaken its seriousness by your manner. [7] open to: given to. [8] quaintly: artfully. [9] taints: faults. [10] unreclaimed: wild.

REYNALDO.
> But, my good lord,—

POLONIUS.
Wherefore should you do this?

REYNALDO.
> Ay, my lord,
I would know that.

POLONIUS.
> Marry, sir, here's my drift;[1]
And, I believe, it is a fetch of warrant.[2]
You laying these slight sullies on my son,
As 'twere a thing a little soil'd i'th'working,
Mark you,
Your party in converse, him you would sound,
Having ever seen in the prenominate[3] crimes
The youth you breathe of guilty, be assured
He closes with you in this consequence;[4]
'Good sir,' or so; or 'friend,' or 'gentleman,'—
According to the phrase, or the addition,[5]
Of man and country.

REYNALDO.
> Very good, my lord.

POLONIUS.
And then, sir, does he this,—he does—What was
I about to say?—By the mass,[6] I was about to say
something:—where did I leave?

REYNALDO.
At 'closes in the consequence,' at 'friend or so,'
and 'gentleman.'

POLONIUS.
At 'closes in the consequence,'—ay, marry;
He closes with you thus: 'I know the gentleman;
I saw him yesterday, or t'other day,

---

drift: meaning. [2] fetch of warrant: guaranteed strategy. [3] prenominate: previously mentioned. [4] He closes with you in this consequence: he agrees with you as follows. [5] addition: title. [6] By the mass: by the Holy mass.

Or then, or then; with such, or such; and, as you say,
There was a' gaming; there o'ertook in's rouse;
There falling out at tennis:' or perchance,
'I saw him enter such a house of sale,'—
Videlicet,[1] a brothel,—or so forth.—
See you now;
Your bait of falsehood takes this carp[2] of truth:
And thus do we of wisdom and of reach,
With windlasses and with assays of bias,[3]
By indirections find directions out:
So, by my former lecture and advice,
Shall you my son. You have me,[4] have you not?

REYNALDO.

My lord, I have.

POLONIUS.

     God be wi' ye! fare ye well.

REYNALDO.

Good my lord!

POLONIUS.

Observe his inclination in yourself.

REYNALDO.

I shall, my lord.

POLONIUS.

And let him ply his music.[5]

REYNALDO.

     Well, my lord.

POLONIUS.

Farewell!   [*Exit* REYNALDO.

Enter OPHELIA.

  How now, Ophelia! what's the matter?

OPHELIA.

O, my lord, my lord, I have been so affrighted!

---

[1] Videlicet: namely; viz.
[2] carp: fish.
[3] windlasses and with assays of bias: roundabout ways.
[4] You have me: you have understood all that I have said?
[5] ply his music: have his way.

POLONIUS.

With what, i'th'name of God?

OPHELIA.

My lord, as I was sewing in my chamber,
Lord Hamlet,—with his doublet all unbraced;[1]
No hat upon his head; his stockings foul'd,
Ungarter'd, and down-gyved[2] to his ancle;
Pale as his shirt; his knees knocking each other;
And with a look so piteous in purport[3]
As if he had been loosed out of hell
To speak of horrors,—he comes before me.

POLONIUS.

Mad for thy love?

OPHELIA.

My lord, I do not know;
But, truly, I do fear it.

POLONIUS.

What said he?

OPHELIA.

He took me by the wrist, and held me hard;
Then goes he to the length of all his arm;
And, with his other hand thus o'er his brow,
He falls to such perusal of my face
As he would draw it. Long stay'd he so;
At last,—a little shaking of mine arm,
And thrice his head thus waving up and down,—
He raised a sigh so piteous and profound,
That it did seem to shatter all his bulk,
And end his being: that done, he lets me go:
And, with his head over his shoulder turn'd,
He seem'd to find his way without his eyes;
For out o' doors he went without their help,
And, to the last, bended[4] their light on me.

---

doublet all unbraced: his coat opened.
down-gyved: hanging down like gyves, or fetters.
purport: meaning.
bended: directed.

POLONIUS.

Come, go with me: I will go seek the king.
This is the very ecstasy of love;
Whose violent property fordoes[1] itself,
And leads the will to desperate undertakings,
As oft as any passion under heaven
That does afflict our natures. I am sorry,—
What, have you given him any hard words of late?

OPHELIA.

No, my good lord; but, as you did command,
I did repel his letters, and denied
His access to me.

POLONIUS.

            That hath made him mad.—
I am sorry that with better heed and judgement
I had not quoted[2] him: I fear'd he did but trifle,
And meant to wrack[3] thee; but, beshrew[4] my jealousy!
It seems it is as proper to our age
To cast beyond ourselves in our opinions,
As it is common for the younger sort
To lack discretion. Come, go we to the king:
This must be known; which, being kept close, might move
More grief to hide than hate to utter love.[5]

Come.   [*Exeunt.*

---

[1] fordoes: kills; destroys. [2] quoted: noted. [3] wrack: torment. [4] beshrew: curse. [5] which, being kept close, might move/More grief to
hide than hate to utter love: that is, to hide Hamlet's actions
would bring more grief to the king and queen than would their
distaste at hearing of Hamlet's love for Ophelia, a girl of lower
rank than he.

SCENE II.

A room in the castle.

Enter KING, QUEEN, ROSENCRANTZ, GUILDENSTERN, *and*
ATTENDANTS.

KING.

Welcome, dear Rosencrantz and Guildenstern!
Moreover that we much did long to see you,
The need we have to use you did provoke
Our hasty sending.[1] Something have you heard
Of Hamlet's transformation; so call it,
Since nor th'exterior nor the inward man
Resembles that it was. What it should be,
More than his father's death, that thus hath put him
So much from th'understanding of himself,
I cannot dream of: I entreat you both,
That, being of so young days brought up with him,
And sith[2] so neighbour'd [3] to his youth and haviour,
That you vouchsafe your rest[4] here in our court
Some little time: so by your companies

---

[1] hasty sending: hasty summons.
[2] sith: since.
[3] neighbour'd: close.
[4] vouchsafe your rest: consent to stay.

To draw him on to pleasures, and to gather,
So much as from occasion you may glean,
Whether aught, to us unknown, afflicts him thus,
That, open'd,[1] lies within our remedy.

QUEEN.

Good gentlemen, he hath much talkt of you;
And sure I am two men there are not living
To whom he more adheres.[2] If it will please you
To show us so much gentry[3] and good will
As to expend your time with us awhile,
For the supply and profit of our hope,
Your visitation shall receive such thanks
As fits a king's remembrance.

ROSENCRANTZ.

                      Both your majesties
Might, by the sovereign power you have of us,
Put your dread pleasures more into command
Than to entreaty.

GUILDENSTERN.

               But we both obey,
And here give up ourselves, in the full bent,[4]
To lay our service freely at your feet,
To be commanded.

KING.

Thanks, Rosencrantz and gentle Guildenstern.

QUEEN.

Thanks, Guildenstern and gentle Rosencrantz:
And I beseech you instantly to visit
My too-much-changed son.—Go, some of you,
And bring these gentlemen where Hamlet is.

GUILDENSTERN.

Heavens make our presence and our practices
Pleasant and helpful to him!

---

[1] opened: revealed.
[2] adheres: is more attached.
[3] gentry: courtesy.
[4] in the full bent: to the limit.

QUEEN.

Ay, amen!

Exeunt ROSENCRANTZ, GUILDENSTERN, *and some* ATTENDANTS.
Enter POLONIUS.

POLONIUS.

Th'ambassadors from Norway, my good lord,
Are joyfully return'd.

KING.

Thou still hast been the father of good news.[1]

POLONIUS.

Have I, my lord? Assure you, my good liege,
I hold my duty, as I hold my soul,
Both to my God and to my gracious king:
And I do think—or else this brain of mine
Hunts not the trail of policy so sure[2]
As it hath used to do—that I have found
The very cause of Hamlet's lunacy.

KING.

O, speak of that; that do I long to hear.

POLONIUS.

Give first admittance to th'ambassadors;
My news shall be the fruit[3] to that great feast.

KING.

Thyself do grace[4] to them, and bring them in.

[*Exit* POLONIUS.

He tells me, my dear Gertrude, he hath found
The head and source of all your son's distemper.

QUEEN.

I doubt it is no other but the main[5]—
His father's death, and our o'erhasty marriage.

KING.

Well, we shall sift[6] him.

---

father of good news: bearer of good tidings.
Hunts not the trail of policy so sure: is not so keen.
fruit: the topping (dessert).
grace: do the honors.
main: dominant cause.
sift: question.

Enter POLONIUS, *with* VOLTIMAND *and* CORNELIUS.

                        Welcome, my good friends!
Say, Voltimand, what from our brother Norway?

    VOLTIMAND.

Most fair return of greetings and desires.
Upon our first, he sent out to suppress
His nephew's levies; which to him appear'd
To be a preparation 'gainst the Polack;[1]
But, better lookt into, he truly found
It was against your highness: whereat grieved,—
That so his sickness, age, and impotence,
Was falsely borne in hand,[2]—sends out arrests
On Fortinbras; which he, in brief, obeys;
Receives rebuke from Norway; and, in fine,[3]
Makes a vow before his uncle never more
To give th'assay of arms against your majesty.[4]
Whereon old Norway, overcome with joy,
Gives him three thousand crowns in annual fee;
And his commission to employ these soldiers,
So levied as before, against the Polack;
With an entreaty, herein further shown,

                              [Gives a paper.

That it might please you to give quiet pass[5]
Through your dominions for this enterprise,
On such regards of safety and allowance
As therein are set down.

    KING.

                        It likes us well;[6]
And at our more consider'd[7] time we'll read,
Answer, and think upon this business.
Meantime we thank you for your well-took labour:

---

[1] the Polack: the Poles. [2] borne in hand: deceived; imposed upon
[3] in fine: finally. [4] To give th'assay of arms against your majesty:
to attempt to bear arms against your country (or majesty). [5] quiet
pass: safe passage. [6] It likes us well: it pleases us. [7] considered:
appropriate.

Go to your rest; at night we'll feast together:
Most welcome home!

> [*Exeunt* VOLTIMAND *and* CORNELIUS.

   POLONIUS.
>   This business is well ended.—

My liege, and madam,—to expostulate[1]
What majesty should be, what duty is,
Why day is day, night night, and time is time,
Were nothing but to waste night, day, and time.
Therefore, since brevity is the soul of wit,
And tediousness the limbs and outward flourishes,
I will be brief:—your noble son is mad:
Mad call I it; for, to define true madness,
What is't but to be nothing else but mad?
But let that go.

   QUEEN.
>   More matter, with less art.[2]

   POLONIUS.

Madam, I swear I use no art at all.
That he is mad, 'tis true: 'tis true, 'tis pity,
And pity 'tis 'tis true: a foolish figure;[3]
But farewell it, for I will use no art.
Mad let us grant him, then: and now remains
That we find out the cause of this effect,—
Or rather say, the cause of this defect,
For this effect defective comes by cause:
Thus it remains, and the remainder thus.
Perpend.[4]
I have a daughter,—have whilst she is mine,—
Who, in her duty and obedience, mark,
Hath given me this: now gather, and surmise.[5]   [*Reads.*

---

[1] expostulate: conjecture.
[2] More matter, with less art: that is, let's get down to facts.
[3] a foolish figure: idle words.
[4] Perpend: consider.
[5] now gather, and surmise: now listen and make up your minds.

To the celestial and my soul's idol, the most beautified
  Ophelia,—

That's an ill phrase, a vile phrase,—'beautified' is a vile phrase:
  but you shall hear. Thus: [*Reads.*

In her excellent white bosom, these, &c.—

    QUEEN.

Came this from Hamlet to her?

    POLONIUS.

Good madam, stay awhile; I will be faithful.   [*Reads.*

                Doubt thou the stars are fire;
                   Doubt that the sun doth move;
                   Doubt truth to be a liar;
                   But never doubt I love.

O dear Ophelia, I am ill at these numbers;[1] I have not art to
  reckon my groans:[2] but that I love thee best, O most best,
  believe it. Adieu.

               Thine evermore, most dear lady, whilst
                  this machine is to him,[3]   HAMLET.

This, in obedience, hath my daughter shown me:
And more above, hath his solicitings,
As they fell out by time, by means, and place,
All given to mine ear.

    KING.

                But how hath she
Receiv'd his love?

    POLONIUS.

               What do you think of me?

    KING.

As of a man faithful and honourable.

    POLONIUS.

I would fain prove so. But what might you think,
When I had seen this hot love on the wing,—

---

[1] **ill at these numbers**: not adept at writing poetry.
[2] **reckon my groans**: express a lover's pangs.
[3] **whilst this machine is to him**: as long as he lives.

As I perceived it, I must tell you that,
Before my daughter told me,—what might you,
Or my dear majesty your queen here, think,
If I had play'd the desk or table-book;[1]
Or given my heart a winking,[2] mute and dumb;
Or lookt upon this love with idle sight;[3]—
What might you think? No, I went round to work,
And my young mistress thus I did bespeak:
'Lord Hamlet is a prince, out of thy star;[4]
This must not be:' and then I prescripts[5] gave her,
That she should lock herself from his resort,[6]
Admit no messengers, receive no tokens.
Which done, she took the fruits of my advice;
And he, repulsed,—a short tale to make,—
Fell into a sadness; then into a fast;
Thence to a watch;[7] thence into a weakness;
Thence to a lightness; and, by this declension,[8]
Into the madness wherein now he raves,
And all we mourn for.

    KING.

                Do you think 'tis this?

    QUEEN.

It may be, very like.

    POLONIUS.

Hath there been such a time—I'ld fain know that—
That I have positively said ''Tis so,'
When it proved otherwise?

    KING.

                Not that I know.

    POLONIUS [*pointing to his head and shoulder*].

Take this from this, if this be otherwise:
If circumstances lead me, I will find

---

[1] **had played the desk or table-book:** had been the confidant.
[2] **given my heart a winking:** i.e., shut his eyes to it. [3] **idle sight:** complacency. [4] **out of thy star:** not in your future. [5] **prescripts:** precepts; advice. [6] **resort:** reach. [7] **watch:** sleepless vigil. [8] **declension:** declining.

Where truth is hid, though it were hid indeed
Within the centre.[1]

KING.

How may we try it further?

POLONIUS.

You know, sometimes he walks four hours together
Here in the lobby.

QUEEN.

So he does, indeed.

POLONIUS.

At such a time I'll loose[2] my daughter to him:
Be you and I behind an arras[3] then;
Mark the encounter: if he love her not,
And be not from his reason faln thereon,
Let me be no assistant for a state,
But keep a farm and carters.[4]

KING.

We will try it.

QUEEN.

But, look, where sadly the poor wretch comes reading.

POLONIUS.

Away, I do beseech you, both away:
I'll board[5] him presently:—O, give me leave.

[*Exeunt* KING, QUEEN, *and* ATTENDANTS.
Enter HAMLET, *reading on a book.*

How does my good Lord Hamlet?

HAMLET.

Well, God-a-mercy.

POLONIUS.

Do you know me, my lord?

HAMLET.

Excellent well; you are a fishmonger.

---

[1] centre: center of the earth. [2] loose: release. [3] arras: wall hanging
or tapestry which gets its name from the town of Arras in Northern
France where it is made. [4] Let me be no assistant for a state,/But
keep a farm and carters: if he has judged the situation wrongly,
then he shouldn't be in his high position, but should, instead, be
a lowly farmer. [5] board: speak to him.

POLONIUS.

Not I, my lord.

HAMLET.

Then I would you were so honest a man.

POLONIUS.

Honest, my lord!

HAMLET.

Ay, sir; to be honest, as this world goes, is to be one man pickt out of ten thousand.

POLONIUS.

That's very true, my lord.

HAMLET.

For if the sun breed maggots in a dead dog, being a god kissing carrion,[1]—Have you a daughter?

POLONIUS.

I have, my lord.

HAMLET.

Let her not walk i' th' sun: conception is a blessing; but not as your daughter may conceive:—friend, look to't.

POLONIUS [*aside*].

How say you by that? Still harping on my daughter:—yet he knew me not at first; he said I was a fishmonger: he is far gone, far gone: and truly in my youth I suffer'd much extremity for love; very near[2] this. I'll speak to him again.— What do you read, my lord?

HAMLET.

Words, words, words.

POLONIUS.

What is the matter, my lord?

HAMLET.

Between who?

---

[1] **a god kissing carrion**: "god" here refers to the sun god, as it was believed the sun bred maggots.
[2] **near**: like.

POLONIUS.

I mean, the matter that you read, my lord.

HAMLET.

Slanders, sir: for the satirical rogue says here, that old men have gray beards; that their faces are wrinkled; their eyes purging thick amber and plum-tree gum; and that they have a plentiful lack of wit, together with most weak hams: all which, sir, though I most powerfully and potently believe, yet I hold it not honesty[1] to have it thus set down; for yourself, sir, shall grow old as I am, if, like a crab, you could go backward.

POLONIUS [*aside*].

Though this be madness, yet there is method in't.—Will you walk out of the air, my lord?

HAMLET.

Into my grave?

POLONIUS.

Indeed, that is out o'th'air.—[*aside*] How pregnant sometimes his replies are! a happiness[2] that often madness hits on, which reason and sanity could not so prosperously be deliver'd of. I will leave him, and suddenly contrive the means of meeting between him and my daughter.—My honourable lord, I will most humbly take my leave of you.

HAMLET.

You cannot, sir, take from me any thing that I will more willingly part withal.—except my life, except my life, except my life.

POLONIUS.

Fare you well, my lord.

---

[1] not honesty: not appropriate.
[2] happiness: a knack.

HAMLET.

These tedious old fools!

Enter ROSENCRANTZ *and* GUILDENSTERN

POLONIUS.

You go to seek the Lord Hamlet; there he is.

ROSENCRANTZ [*to* POLONIUS].

God save you, sir!   [*Exit* POLONIUS.

GUILDENSTERN.

My honour'd lord!

ROSENCRANTZ.

My most dear lord!

HAMLET.

My excellent good friends! How dost thou, Guildenstern? Ah, Rosencrantz! Good lads, how do ye both?

ROSENCRANTZ.

As the indifferent[1] children of the earth.

GUILDENSTERN.

Happy, in that we are not overhappy;
On Fortune's cap we are not the very button.

HAMLET.

Nor the soles of her shoe?

ROSENCRANTZ.

Neither, my lord.

HAMLET.

Then you live about her waist, or in the middle of her favours?

GUILDENSTERN.

Faith, her privates we.

HAMLET.

In the secret parts of Fortune? O, most true; she is a strumpet.[2] What's the news?

ROSENCRANTZ.

None, my lord, but that the world's grown honest.

---

[1] indifferent: average.
[2] strumpet: a fickle woman.

HAMLET.

Then is doomsday near: but your news is not true. Let me question more in particular: what have you, my good friends, deserved at the hands of Fortune, that she sends you to prison hither?

GUILDENSTERN.

Prison, my lord!

HAMLET.

Denmark's a prison.

ROSENCRANTZ.

Then is the world one.

HAMLET.

A goodly one; in which there are many confines, wards, and dungeons,[1] Denmark being one o'th' worst.

ROSENCRANTZ.

We think not so, my lord.

HAMLET.

Why, then, 'tis none to you: for there is nothing either good or bad, but thinking makes it so: to me it is a prison.

ROSENCRANTZ.

Why, then, your ambition makes it one; 'tis too narrow for your mind.

HAMLET.

O God, I could be bounded in a nut-shell, and count myself a king of infinite space, were it not that I have bad dreams.

GUILDENSTERN.

Which dreams, indeed, are ambition; for the very substance of the ambitious is merely the shadow of a dream.

---

[1] confines, wards, and/dungeons: prison cells.

HAMLET.

A dream itself is but a shadow.

ROSENCRANTZ.

Truly, and I hold ambition of so airy and light a quality, that
it is but a shadow's shadow.

HAMLET.

Then are our beggars bodies, and our monarchs and out-
stretcht heroes the beggars' shadows.
Shall we to th'court? for, by my fay,[1] I cannot reason.

ROSENCRANTZ *and* GUILDENSTERN.

We'll wait upon[2] you.

HAMLET.

No such matter: I will not sort[3] you with the rest of my
servants; for, to speak to you like an honest man, I am most
dreadfully attended. But, in the beaten way of friendship,[4]
what make you at Elsinore?

ROSENCRANTZ.

To visit you, my lord; no other occasion.

HAMLET.

Beggar that I am, I am even poor in thanks; but I thank you:
and sure, dear friends, my thanks are too dear a halfpenny.[5]
Were you not sent for? Is it your own inclining?[6] Is it a free
visitation? Come, deal justly[7] with me: come, come; nay,
speak.

GUILDENSTERN.

What should we say, my lord?

HAMLET.

Why, any thing—but to the purpose. You were sent for; and
there is a kind of confession in your looks, which your modes-
ties have not craft enough to colour:[8] I know the good king
and queen have sent for you.

---

[1] fay: faith. [2] wait upon: that is, go with Hamlet, although Hamlet
decides to take the words literally. [3] sort: class. [4] beaten way of
friendship: as old friends. [5] too dear a halfpenny: not worth a
halfpenny. [6] inclining: will. [7] justly: openly. [8] colour: hide.

ROSENCRANTZ.

To what end, my lord?

HAMLET.

That you must teach me. But let me conjure you, by the
rights of our fellowship, by the consonancy of our youth, by
the obligation of our ever-preserved love, and by what more
dear[1] a better proposer could charge you withal, be even and
direct[2] with me, whether you were sent for, or no.

ROSENCRANTZ [*aside to* GUILDENSTERN].

What say you?

HAMLET [*aside*].

Nay, then, I have an eye of[3] you.—If you love me, hold not
off.

GUILDENSTERN.

My lord, we were sent for.

HAMLET.

I will tell you why; so shall my anticipation prevent your dis-
covery, and your secrecy to the king and queen moult no
feather.[4] I have of late—but wherefore I know not—lost all
my mirth, forgone all custom of exercises; and, indeed, it
goes so heavily with my disposition that this goodly frame,
the earth, seems to me a sterile promontory; this most excellent canopy, the air, look you, this brave o'erhanging
firmament, this majestical roof fretted with golden fire,[5]—
why, it appears no other thing to me than a foul and pestilent congregation of vapours. What a piece of work is man!
how noble in reason! how infinite in faculty! in form and
moving how express[6] and admirable! in action how like an
angel! in apprehension how like a god! the beauty of the

---

[1] dear: worthy.
[2] even and direct: honest.
[3] of: on.
[4] moult no feather: remain unchanged.
[5] fretted with golden fire: dotted or ornamented with stars.
[6] express: precise; fitted to its purpose.

world! the paragon of animals! And yet, to me, what is this quintessence of dust? man delights not me; no, nor woman either, though by your smiling you seem to say so.

ROSENCRANTZ.

My lord, there was no such stuff in my thoughts.

HAMLET.

Why did you laugh, then, when I said 'man delights not me'?

ROSENCRANTZ.

To think, my lord, if you delight not in man, what lenten[1] entertainment the players shall receive from you: we coted[2] them on the way; and hither are they coming, to offer you service.

HAMLET.

He that plays the king shall be welcome,—his majesty shall have tribute of me; the adventurous knight shall use his foil and target;[3] the lover shall not sigh gratis;[4] the humorous man shall end his part in peace;[5] the clown shall make those laugh whose lungs are tickle o'th'sere;[6] and the lady shall say her mind freely, or the blank verse shall halt for't.—What players are they?

ROSENCRANTZ.

Even those you were wont to take such delight in, the tragedians of the city.

HAMLET.

How chances it they travel? their residence,[7] both in reputation and profit, was better both ways.

ROSENCRANTZ.

I think their inhibition comes by the means of the late innovation.[8]

---

[1] lenten: poor; scanty. [2] coted: passed. [3] foil and target: sword and shield. [4] gratis: in vain. [5] the humorous/man shall end his part in peace: the actor shall be allowed to give his performance. [6] tickle o'th'sere: quick on the trigger. [7] their residence: their stay in the city. [8] late innovation: the recent fad of acting companies composed of boys.

HAMLET.

Do they hold the same estimation they did when I was in t
city? are they so follow'd?

ROSENCRANTZ.

No, indeed, they are not.

HAMLET.

How comes it? do they grow rusty?

ROSENCRANTZ.

Nay, their endeavour keeps in the wonted pace: but there
sir, an aery[1] of children, little eyases,[2] that cry out on the to
of question, and are most tyrannically clapt[3] for't: these a
now the fashion; and so berattle[4] the common stages,—
they call them,—that many wearing rapiers are afraid
goose-quills, and dare scarce come thither.

HAMLET.

What, are they children? who maintains 'em? how are the
escoted?[5] Will they pursue the quality no longer than the
can sing?[6] will they not say afterwards, if they should gro
themselves to common players,—as it is most like, if the
means are no better,—their writers do them wrong, to mak
them exclaim against their own succession?

ROSENCRANTZ.

Faith, there has been much to do on both sides; and th
nation holds it no sin to tarre[7] them to controversy; there wa
for a while, no money bid for argument, unless the poet an
the player went to cuffs[8] in the question.

HAMLET.

Is't possible?

GUILDENSTERN.

O, there has been much throwing about of brains.

---

[1] aery: brood or nest. [2] little eyases: young hawks. [3] tyrannicall
clapt: applauded extravagantly. [4] berattle: scold at. [5] escoted: sup
ported; that is, what profession or calling do they follow. [6] pursu
the quality no longer than they/can sing: will they pursue actin
when they lose their soprano voices. [7] tarre: urge on; incite. [8]
cuffs: to blows.

HAMLET.

Do the boys carry it away? [1]

ROSENCRANTZ.

Ay, that they do, my lord; Hercules[2] and his load too.

HAMLET.

It is not very strange; for my uncle is king of Denmark, and those that would make mows[3] at him while my father lived, give twenty, forty, fifty, an hundred ducats a-piece for his picture in little.[4] 'Sblood, there is something in this more than natural, if philosophy could find it out.

[Flourish of trumpets within.

GUILDENSTERN.

There are the players.

HAMLET.

Gentlemen, you are welcome to Elsinore. Your hands, come: the appurtenance[5] of welcome is fashion and ceremony: let me comply with you in this garb,[6] lest my extent[7] to the players, which, I tell you, must show fairly outward, should more appear like entertainment than yours. You are welcome: but my uncle-father and aunt-mother are deceived.

GUILDENSTERN.

In what, my dear lord?

HAMLET.

I am but mad north-north-west: when the wind is southerly I know a hawk from a handsaw.[8]

Enter POLONIUS.

POLONIUS.

Well be with you, gentlemen!

---

[1] **carry it away:** are they able to put the play across? [2] **Hercules:** Atlas carrying the world on his shoulders. [3] **mows:** grimaces. [4] **picture in little:** miniature. [5] **appurtenance:** adjunct. [6] **this garb:** this fashion. [7] **extent:** show of courtesy. [8] **I am but mad north-north-west; when the wind is southerly,/I know a hawk from a handsaw:** that is, when it suits his purpose, Hamlet puts on an act of madness.

HAMLET.

Hark you, Guildenstern;—and you too;—at each ear a hearer: that great baby you see there is not yet out of his swaddling-clouts.[1]

ROSENCRANTZ.

Happily[2] he's the second time come to them; for they say an old man is twice a child.

HAMLET.

I will prophesy he comes to tell me of the players; mark it.— You say right, sir: o' Monday morning; 'twas then, indeed.

POLONIUS.

My lord, I have news to tell you.

HAMLET.

My lord, I have news to tell you. When Roscius[3] was an actor in Rome,—

POLONIUS.

The actors are come hither, my lord.

HAMLET.

Buz, buz!

POLONIUS.

Upon mine honour,—

HAMLET.

Then came each actor on his ass,—

POLONIUS.

The best actors in the world, either for tragedy, comedy, history, pastoral, pastoral-comical, historical-pastoral, tragical-historical, tragical-comical-historical-pastoral, scene individable, or poem unlimited: Seneca[4] cannot be too heavy, nor Plautus[5] too light. For the law of writ and the liberty, these are the only men.

---

[1] swaddling-clouts: swaddling clothes.
[2] Happily: perhaps.
[3] Roscius: a Roman actor, so famous that his name came to mean a successful actor.
[4] Seneca: a Roman playwright.
[5] Plautus: a great comic dramatist of ancient Rome.

HAMLET.

O Jephthah, judge of Israel, what a treasure hadst thou!

POLONIUS.

What a treasure had he, my lord?

HAMLET.

Why,

> 'One fair daughter, and no more,
>   The which he loved passing[1] well.'

POLONIUS [aside].

Still on my daughter.

HAMLET.

Am I not i'th'right, old Jephthah?

POLONIUS.

If you call me Jephthah, my lord, I have a daughter that I love passing well.

HAMLET.

Nay, that follows not.

POLONIUS.

What follows, then, my lord?

HAMLET.

Why,

> 'As by lot, God wot,'

and then, you know,

> 'It came to pass, as most like it was,'—

the first row of the pious chanson will show you more; for look, where my abridgement[2] comes.

Enter four or five PLAYERS.

You are welcome, masters; welcome, all; I am glad to see thee well; welcome, good friends.—O, my old friend! Why, thy face is valanced[3] since I saw thee last; comest thou to beard me in Denmark?—What, my young lady and mistress! By'r lady, your ladyship is nearer to heaven than when I saw you last by

---

passing: surpassingly.
abridgement: a short play.
valanced: bearded.

the altitude of a chopine.[1] Pray God, your voice, like a piec
of uncurrent gold,[2] be not crackt within the ring.—Master
you are welcome. We'll e'en to't[3] like French falconers, fly a
any thing we see: we'll have a speech straight:[4] come, giv
us a taste of your quality;[5] come, a passionate speech.

FIRST PLAYER.

What speech, my good lord?

HAMLET.

I heard thee speak me a speech once,—but it was never acted
or, if it was, not above once; for the play, I remember, please
not the million; 'twas caviare to the general:[6] but it was—a
I received it, and others, whose judgements in such matter
cried in the top of mine[7]—an excellent play, well digested i
the scenes, set down with as much modesty as cunning. I re
member, one said there were no sallets[8] in the lines to mak
the matter savoury, nor no matter in the phrase that migh
indict the author of affection:[9] but call'd it an honest method
as wholesome as sweet, and by very much more handsom
than fine. One speech in it I chiefly loved: 'twas Aeneas'[10] tal
to Dido;[11] and thereabout of it especially where he speaks o
Priam's[12] slaughter: if it live in your memory, begin at thi
line;—let me see, let me see;

    'The rugged Pyrrhus,[13] like th'Hycanian beast,'[14]

—'tis not so:—it begins with Pyrrhus;

    'The rugged Pyrrhus,—he whose sable arms,
    Black as his purpose, did the night resemble
    When he lay couched in the ominous horse,—
    Hath now this dread and black complexion smear'd

---

[1] **chopine:** a high shoe or clog. [2] **uncurrent gold:** not negotiable
[3] **e'en to't:** take to it. [4] **straight:** right away. [5] **quality:** ability
[6] **caviare to the general:** above the tastes of the masses. [7] **cried in
the top of mine:** that is, their judgment surpassed Hamlet's.
[8] **sallets:** salads; spicy passages. [9] **affection:** affectation. [10] **Aeneas:**
hero of the *Iliad*. [11] **Dido:** Queen of Carthage. [12] **Priam:** King of
Troy. [13] **Pyrrhus:** son of Achilles. [14] **Hyrcanian beast:** tiger from
Hyrcania, a territory lying south of the Caspian Sea and noted for
its tigers.

With heraldry more dismal; head to foot
Now is he total gules;[1] horridly trickt[2]
With blood of fathers, mothers, daughters, sons,
Baked and impasted [3] with the parching streets,
That lend a tyrannous and damned light
To their vile murders: roasted in wrath and fire,
And thus o'er-sized [4] with coagulate gore,
With eyes like carbuncles,[5] the hellish Pyrrhus
Old grandsire Priam seeks.'—
So, proceed you.

POLONIUS.

'Fore God, my lord, well spoken, with good accent and good
discretion.

FIRST PLAYER.

          'Anon he finds him
Striking too short at Greeks; his antique sword,
Rebellious to his arm, lies where it falls,
Repugnant[6] to command; unequal matcht,
Pyrrhus at Priam drives; in rage strikes wide;
But with the whiff and wind of his fell [7] sword
Th'unnerved father falls. Then senseless Ilium,[8]
Seeming to feel this blow, with flaming top
Stoops to his base; and with a hideous crash
Takes prisoner Pyrrhus' ear: for, lo! his sword,
Which was declining on the milky head
Of reverend Priam, seem'd i'th'air to stick:
So, as a painted tyrant,[9] Pyrrhus stood;
And, like a neutral to his[10] will and matter,
Did nothing.
But, as we often see, against some storm,

---

total gules: all red; gules is the color red in heraldry. [2] trickt:
decorated. [3] impasted: imprinted. [4] Oer-sized: glazed. [5] carbuncles:
red sores. [6] Repugnant: rebellious. [7] fell: deadly. [8] Illium: fortified
battlements of Troy. [9] as a painted tyrant: as motionless as a
painting. [10] his: its.

A silence in the heavens, the rack[1] stand still,
The bold winds speechless, and the orb[2] below
As hush as death, anon the dreadful thunder
Doth rend the region;[3] so, after Pyrrhus' pause,
Aroused vengeance sets him new a-work;
And never did the Cyclops' [4] hammers fall
On Mars[5] his armour, forged for proof eterne,[6]
With less remorse than Pyrrhus' bleeding sword
Now falls on Priam.—
Out, out, thou strumpet, Fortune! All you gods,
In general synod, take away her power;
Break all the spokes and fellies[7] from her wheel,
And bowl the round nave[8] down the hill of heaven,
As low as to the fiends!' [9]

POLONIUS.

This is too long.

HAMLET.

It shall to th'barber's, with your beard.—Prithee, say on:—he's
for a jig or a tale of bawdry, or he sleeps:—say on: come to
Hecuba.[10]

FIRST PLAYER.

'But who, O, who had seen the mobled [11] queen—'

HAMLET.

'The mobled queen'?

POLONIUS.

That's good; 'mobled queen' is good.

FIRST PLAYER.

'Run barefoot up and down, threat'ning the flames
With bisson rheum;[12] a clout[13] upon that head
Where late the diadem stood; and for a robe,

---

[1] rack: clouds. [2] orb: the earth. [3] region: upper air. [4] the Cyclops:
the one-eyed giants in Greek Mythology who assisted Vulcan, the
god of destructive fire (blacksmith). [5] Mars: the god of war. [6] proof
eterne: to last forever. [7] fellies: the sections forming the rim of a
wheel. [8] nave: hub. [9] to the fiends: hell. [10] Hecuba: wife of Priam.
[11] mobled: muffled. [12] bisson rheum: blinding tears. [13] clout: cloth.

About her lank and all o'er-teemed [1] loins,
A blanket, in th'alarm of fear caught up;—
Who this had seen, with tongue in venom steept,
'Gainst Fortune's state would treason have
    pronounced;[2]
But if the gods themselves did see her then,
When she saw Pyrrhus make malicious sport
In mincing with his sword her husband's limbs,
The instant burst of clamour that she made—
Unless things mortal move them not at all—
Would have made milch[3] the burning eyes of heaven,
And passion in the gods.'

POLONIUS.

Look, whe'r[4] he has not turn'd his colour, and has tears in's
eyes.—Pray you, no more.

HAMLET.

'Tis well; I'll have thee speak out the rest soon.—Good my
lord, will you see the players well bestow'd?[5] Do you hear,
let them be well used;[6] for they are the abstract and brief
chronicles of the time: after your death you were better have
a bad epitaph than their ill report while you live.

POLONIUS.

My lord, I will use them according to their desert.

HAMLET.

God's bodykins,[7] man, better: use every man after his desert,
and who should scape[8] whipping? Use them after your own
honour and dignity: the less they deserve, the more merit is
in your bounty. Take them in.

---

[1] o'er-teemed: spent. [2] Gainst Fortune's state would treason have/
pronounced: would have rebelled against Fortune's rule. [3] milch:
flowing as with milk; weeping. [4] whe'r: whether. [5] bestow'd: put
up; accommodated. [6] used: treated. [7] God's bodykins: God's little
children. [8] scape: escape.

POLONIUS.

Come, sirs.

HAMLET.

Follow him, friends: we'll hear a play to-morrow.
[*Exit* POLONIUS *with all the* PLAYERS *but the First.*] Dost thou
hear me, old friend; can you play the Murder of Gonzago?

FIRST PLAYER.

Ay, my lord.

HAMLET.

We'll ha't to-morrow night. You could, for a need, study a
speech of some dozen or sixteen lines, which I would set
down and insert in't, could you not?

FIRST PLAYER.

Ay, my lord.

HAMLET.

Very well.—Follow that lord; and look you mock him not.
[*Exit* FIRST PLAYER.] My good friends, I'll leave you till
night: you are welcome to Elsinore.

ROSENCRANTZ.

Good my lord!

HAMLET.

Ay, so, God be wi' ye! [*Exeunt* ROSENCRANTZ *and* GUILDEN-
STERN.] Now I am alone.
O, what a rogue and peasant slave am I!
Is it not monstrous, that this player here,
But in a fiction, in a dream of passion,
Could force his soul so to his own conceit,[1]
That, from her working, all his visage wann'd;[2]
Tears in his eyes, distraction in's aspect,[3]
A broken voice, and his whole function suiting

---

[1] to his own conceit: the idea he had conceived.
[2] visage wann'd: his face paled.
[3] distraction in's aspect: distracted appearance.

With forms to his conceit? and all for nothing!
For Hecuba!
What's Hecuba to him, or he to Hecuba,
That he should weep for her? What would he do,
Had he the motive and the cue[1] for passion
That I have? He would drown the stage with tears,
And cleave the general ear[2] with horrid speech;
Make mad the guilty, and appal the free,[3]
Confound the ignorant; and amaze, indeed,
The very faculties of eyes and ears.
Yet I,
A dull and muddy-mettled rascal,[4] peak,
Like John-a-dreams,[5] unpregnant of[6] my cause,
And can say nothing; no, not for a king,
Upon whose property and most dear life
A damn'd defeat[7] was made. Am I a coward?
Who calls me villain? breaks my pate[8] across?
Plucks off my beard, and blows it in my face?
Tweaks me by the'nose? gives me the lie i'th'throat,
As deep as to the lungs? who does me this, ha?
'Swounds,[9] I should take it: for it cannot be
But I am pigeon-liver'd,[10] and lack gall
To make oppression bitter;[11] or, ere this,
I should have fatted all the region kites[12]
With this slave's offal:—bloody, bawdy villain!
Remorseless, treacherous, lecherous, kindless villain!
O, vengeance!
Why, what an ass am I! This is most brave,
That I, the son of a dear father murder'd,

---

[1] **cue:** reason. [2] **general ear:** the audience. [3] **free:** free of guilt; the innocent. [4] **muddy-mettled rascal:** dull-spirited fellow. [5] **peak/Like John-a-dreams:** mope like a daydreamer. [6] **unpregnant of:** unmoved by. [7] **damn'd defeat:** utter destruction. [8] **pate:** head. [9] **'Swounds:** God's wounds. [10] **pigeon-liver'd:** timid. [11] **To make oppression bitter:** to resist oppression. [12] **region kites:** hawklike birds of the air (scavengers).

Prompted to my revenge by heaven and hell,
Must, like a whore, unpack[1] my heart with words,
And fall a-cursing, like a very drab,[2]
A scullion! [3]
Fie upon't! foh!—About, my brain! I have heard
That guilty creatures sitting at a play
Have by the very cunning[4] of the scene
Been struck so to the soul, that presently
They have proclaim'd their malefactions;
For murder, though it have no tongue, will speak
With most miraculous organ. I'll have these players
Play something like the murder of my father
Before mine uncle: I'll observe his looks;
I'll tent[5] him to the quick: if he but blench,[6]
I know my course. The spirit that I have seen
May be the devil: and the devil hath power
T'assume a pleasing shape; yea, and perhaps
Out of my weakness and my melancholy,
As he is very potent with such spirits,[7]
Abuses[8] me to damn me: I'll have grounds
More relative[9] than this:—the play's the thing
Wherein I'll catch the conscience of the king.   [*Exit.*

---

[1] **unpack**: unburden. [2] **drab**: a low woman. [3] **scullion**: kitchen help.
[4] **cunning**: skill. [5] **tent**: probe. [6] **blench**: blanch; pale. [7] **spirits**:
moods. [8] **Abuses**: deceives. [9] **relative**: applicable.

Hamlet

ACT 3

ACT III

OPHELIA MEETS Hamlet while Polonius and Claudius observe them unseen. At first gentle to her, Hamlet senses he is being spied upon, rails against Ophelia and all women, then makes a veiled threat against the life of Claudius. Claudius, not convinced that Hamlet is a distraught lover, nevertheless agrees to postpone drastic action until the Queen has had a chance to speak with Hamlet. The play is performed, and at the crucial moment Claudius flees from the hall, assuring Hamlet of his guilt. The Prince does nothing immediately, however. Summoned to his mother's bedroom, he comes by accident upon Claudius, who is kneeling in prayer. Hamlet, on the verge of killing him, decides instead to wait for a time when he can be certain that Claudius' soul will be damned. He goes to his mother's closet, where Polonius has hidden himself. The old man, thinking Hamlet is going to kill Gertrude, cries out, and Hamlet, mistaking him for Claudius, plunges his sword through the arras and kills him. The ghost, visible only to Hamlet, reappears and causes him further remorse. After enjoining his mother to keep his secret, Hamlet carries the body of Polonius to another room.

ACT III. Scene I.

Elsinore. A room in the castle.

Enter KING, QUEEN, POLONIUS, OPHELIA, ROSENCRANTZ, *and*
GUILDENSTERN.

KING.
And can you, by no drift of circumstance,[1]
Get from him why he puts on this confusion,[2]
Grating so harshly all his days of quiet
With turbulent and dangerous lunacy?

ROSENCRANTZ.
He does confess he feels himself distracted;
But from what cause he will by no means speak.

---

drift of circumstance: direction of conversation.
this confusion: this pretension of madness.

GUILDENSTERN.

Nor do we find him forward to be sounded;[1]
But, with a crafty madness, keeps aloof,
When we would bring him on to some confession
Of his true state.

QUEEN.

        Did he receive you well?

ROSENCRANTZ.

Most like a gentleman.

GUILDENSTERN.

But with much forcing of his disposition.

ROSENCRANTZ.

Niggard [2] of question; but, of our demands,[3]
Most free in his reply.

QUEEN.

        Did you assay him
To any pastime? [4]

ROSENCRANTZ.

Madam, it so fell out, that certain players
We o'er-raught[5] on the way: of these we told him;
And there did seem in him a kind of joy
To hear of it: they are about the court;
And, as I think, they have already order[6]
This night to play before him.

POLONIUS.

        'Tis most true:
And he beseecht me to entreat your majesties
To hear and see the matter.[7]

---

[1] forward to be sounded: willing to be questioned. [2] Niggard: spare.
[3] demands: questions. [4] assay him/To any pastime: did you try to
interest him in any pastime? [5] o'er-raught: overtook. [6] order: plans.
[7] the matter: the play.

KING.

With all my heart; and it doth much content[1] me
To hear him so inclined.—
Good gentlemen, give him a further edge,[2]
And drive his purpose on to these delights.

ROSENCRANTZ.

We shall, my lord.

[*Exeunt* ROSENCRANTZ *and* GUILDENSTERN.

KING.

                    Sweet Gertrude, leave us too;
For we have closely[3] sent for Hamlet hither,
That he, as 'twere by accident, may here
Affront[4] Ophelia;
Her father and myself—lawful espials[5]—
Will so bestow[6] ourselves that, seeing, unseen,
We may of their encounter frankly judge;
And gather by him, as he is behaved,
If 't be th'affliction of his love or no
That thus he suffers for.

QUEEN.

                    I shall obey you:—
And for your part, Ophelia, I do wish
That your good beauties be the happy cause
Of Hamlet's wildness: so shall I hope your virtues
Will bring him to his wonted way[7] again,
To both your honours.

OPHELIA.

                    Madam, I wish it may   [*Exit* QUEEN.

POLONIUS.

Ophelia, walk you here.—Gracious, so please you,
We will bestow ourselves.—[*to* OPHELIA] Read on this book;

---

[1] content: please. [2] give him a further edge: sharpen his interest.
[3] closely: secretly. [4] Affront: meet. [5] espials: spies. [6] bestow: place.
[7] wonted way: the way he used to be.

That show of such an exercise may colour
Your loneliness.[1]—We are oft to blame in this,—
'Tis too much proved,—that with devotion's visage
And pious action we do sugar o'er
The devil himself.

    KING [*aside*].
                     O, 'tis too true!
How smart a lash that speech doth give my conscience!
The harlot's cheek, beautied with plastering art,[2]
Is not more ugly to the thing that helps it
Than is my deed to my most painted word:[3]
O heavy burden!

    POLONIUS.
I hear him coming: let's withdraw, my lord.

                  [*Exeunt* KING *and* POLONIU

         Enter HAMLET

    HAMLET.
To be, or not to be,—that is the question:—
Whether 'tis nobler in the mind to suffer
The slings and arrows of outrageous fortune,
Or to take arms against a sea of troubles,
And by opposing end them?—To die,—to sleep,—
No more; and by a sleep to say we end
The heart-ache, and the thousand natural shocks
That flesh is heir to, 'tis a consummation
Devoutly to be wisht. To die,—to sleep;—
To sleep! perchance to dream: ay, there's the rub;
For in that sleep of death what dreams may come,
When we have shuffled off this mortal coil,[4]

---

[1] may color/Your loneliness: may give reason for your being alon[e]
[2] plastering art: make-up.
[3] most painted word: most flowery and misleading word.
[4] When we have shuffled off this mortal coil: when we have free[d]
ourselves from this earthly turmoil.

Must give us pause: there's the respect[1]
That makes calamity of so long life;
For who would bear the whips and scorns of time,
The oppressor's wrong, the proud man's contumely,[2]
The pangs of despised [3] love, the law's delay,
The insolence of office,[4] and the spurns[5]
That patient merit of the unworthy takes,
When he himself might his quietus[6] make
With a bare bodkin? [7] who would fardels[8] bear,
To grunt and sweat under a weary life,
But that the dread of something after death,—
The undiscover'd country, from whose bourn[9]
No traveller returns,—puzzles the will,
And makes us rather bear those ills we have
Than fly to others that we know not of?
Thus conscience does make cowards of us all;
And thus the native hue of resolution[10]
Is sicklied o'er with the pale cast of thought;[11]
And enterprises of great pith and moment,[12]
With this regard,[13] their currents turn awry,
And lose the name of action.—Soft you now!
The fair Ophelia!—Nymph, in thy orisons[14]
Be all my sins remember'd.

    OPHELIA.

                     Good my lord,
How does your honour for this many a day?

    HAMLET.

I humbly thank you; well, well, well.

    OPHELIA.

My lord, I have remembrances of yours,
That I have longed long to re-deliver;
I pray you, now receive them.

---

[1] respect: consideration. [2] contumely: humiliation. [3] despised: rejected. [4] office: high office. [5] spurns: insults. [6] quietus: release through death. [7] bare bodkin: unsheathed dagger. [8] fardels: burdens. [9] bourn: boundaries. [10] native hue of resolution: natural strength and purpose of resolution. [11] Is sicklied o'er with the pale cast of thought: is weakened by thought. [12] pith and moment: importance. [13] regard: consideration. [14] orisons: prayers.

HAMLET.

No, not I;

I never gave you aught.

OPHELIA.

My honour'd lord, you know right well you did;
And, with them, words of so sweet breath[1] composed
As made the things more rich: their perfume lost,
Take these again; for to the noble mind
Rich gifts wax[2] poor when givers prove unkind.
There, my lord.

HAMLET.

Ha, ha! are you honest?

OPHELIA.

My lord?

HAMLET.

Are you fair?

OPHELIA.

What means your lordship?

HAMLET.

That if you be honest and fair, your honesty should admit no
discourse to your beauty.

OPHELIA.

Could beauty, my lord, have better commerce than with
honesty?

HAMLET.

Ay, truly; for the power of beauty will sooner transform
honesty from what it is to a bawd than the force of honesty
can translate beauty into his likeness: this was sometime[3] a
paradox, but now the time gives it proof. I did love you once.

OPHELIA.

Indeed, my lord, you made me believe so.

---

[1] breath: meaning.
[2] wax: grow.
[3] sometime: formerly.

HAMLET.

You should not have believed me; for virtue cannot so in-
oculate our old stock, but we shall relish of it:[1] I loved you
not.

OPHELIA.

I was the more deceived.

HAMLET.

Get thee to a nunnery: why wouldst thou be a breeder of
sinners? I am myself indifferent honest:[2] but yet I could
accuse me of such things, that it were better my mother had
not borne me: I am very proud, revengeful, ambitious; with
more offences at my beck[3] than I have thoughts to put them
in, imagination to give them shape, or time to act them in.
What should such fellows as I do crawling between earth and
heaven? We are arrant knaves, all; believe none of us. Go thy
ways to a nunnery. Where's your father?

OPHELIA.

At home, my lord.

HAMLET.

Let the doors be shut upon him, that he may play the fool
no where but in's own house. Farewell.

OPHELIA.

O, help him, you sweet heavens!

HAMLET.

If thou dost marry, I'll give thee this plague[4] for thy dowry,—
be thou as chaste as ice, as pure as snow, thou shalt not
escape calumny.[5] Get thee to a nunnery, go: farewell. Or, if
thou wilt needs marry, marry a fool; for wise men know well
enough what monsters you make of them. To a nunnery, go;
and quickly too. Farewell.

---

[1] virtue cannot so in-/oculate our old stock, but we shall relish of
it: virtue cannot alter our innate meanness.
[2] indifferent honest: moderately honest.
[3] offences at my beck: sins that I can recall.
[4] plague: curse.
[5] calumny: slander.

OPHELIA.

O heavenly powers, restore him! [1]

HAMLET.

I have heard of your paintings too, well enough; God has given you one face, and you make yourselves another: you jig, you amble, and you lisp, and nickname God's creatures, and make your wantonness[2] your ignorance. Go to, I'll no more on't; it hath made me mad. I say, we will have no more marriages: those that are married already, all but one, shall live; the rest shall keep as they are. To a nunnery, go. [*Exit.*

OPHELIA.

O, what a noble mind is here o'erthrown!
The courtier's, soldier's, scholar's eye, tongue, sword;
Th'expectancy and rose of the fair state,[3]
The glass of fashion[4] and the mould of form,[5]
Th'observ'd of all observers,—quite, quite down!
And I, of ladies most dejected and wretched,
That suckt the honey of his music vows,
Now see that noble and most sovereign reason,
Like sweet bells jangled, out of tune and harsh;
That unmatcht form and feature of blown youth[6]
Blasted with ectasy:[7] O, woe is me
T'have seen what I have seen, see what I see!

Enter KING *and* POLONIUS.

KING.

Love! his affections do not that way tend;
Nor what he spake, though it lackt form a little,
Was not like madness. There's something in his soul

---

[1] **restore him:** restore his senses. [2] **wantonness:** willfulness.
[3] **Th'expectancy and rose of the fair state:** the heir and chief adornment of the state of Denmark. [4] **glass of fashion:** mirror or model of fashion. [5] **mold of form:** model of behavior. [6] **blown youth:** full manhood; the bloom of youth. [7] **ecstasy:** madness.

O'er which his melancholy sits on brood;
And I do doubt the hatch and the disclose[1]
Will be some danger: which for to prevent,
I have in quick determination
Thus set it down:—he shall with speed to England,
For the demand of our neglected tribute:
Haply,[2] the seas, and countries different,
With variable objects, shall expel
This something-settled[3] matter in his heart;
Whereon his brains still beating puts him thus
From fashion of himself.[4] What think you on't?

    POLONIUS.

It shall do well: but yet do I believe
The origin and commencement of his grief
Sprung from neglected love.—How now, Ophelia!
You need not tell us what Lord Hamlet said;
We heard it all.—My lord, do as you please;
But, if you hold it fit, after the play,
Let his queen mother all alone entreat him
To show his grief: let her be round[5] with him;
And I'll be placed, so please you, in the ear
Of all their conference.[6] If she find him not,
To England send him; or confine him where
Your wisdom best shall think.

    KING.

                  It shall be so:
Madness in great ones must not unwatched go.   [Exeunt.

---

[1] the hatch and the disclose: the outcome. [2] haply: by chance.
[3] something-settled: fixed. [4] From fashion of himself: from being
his old self. [5] round: forthright; direct. [6] And I'll be placed, so
please you, in the ear/Of all their conference: hidden within
earshot.

SCENE II.

A hall in the castle.

Enter HAMLET *and two or three of the* PLAYERS.

HAMLET.

Speak the speech, I pray you, as I pronounced it to you,
trippingly on the tongue: but if you mouth it, as many of your
players do, I had as lief the town-crier spoke my lines. Nor
do not saw the air too much with your hand, thus; but use
all gently: for in the very torrent, tempest, and, as I may
say, the whirlwind of passion, you must acquire and beget a
temperance that may give it smoothness. O, it offends me to
the soul to hear a robustious periwig-pated fellow tear a
passion to tatters, to very rags, to split the ears of the groundlings,[1] who, for the most part, are capable of nothing but
inexplicable dumb-shows and noise: I would have such a
fellow whipt for o'erdoing Termagant;[2] it out-herods Herod:[3]
pray you, avoid it.

FIRST PLAYER.

I warrant your honour.

HAMLET.

Be not too tame[4] neither, but let your own discretion be your
tutor: suit the action to the word, the word to the action; with
this special observance, that you o'erstep not the modesty[5] of
nature: for any thing so overdone is from the purpose of playing, whose end, both at the first and now, was and is, to hold,
as 'twere, the mirror up to nature; to show virtue her own feature, scorn her own image, and the very age and body of the
time his form and pressure.[6] Now, this overdone, or come

---

[1] groundlings: the lowest of the spectators; that is, those who stood
in the yard. [2] Termagant: a ranting character in old plays. [3] Herod:
a highly dramatic part. [4] tame: restrained. [5] modesty: limits (of
nature). [6] pressure: impression.

tardy off,[1] though it make the unskilful [2] laugh, cannot but make the judicious grieve; the censure[3] of the which one must, in your allowance,[4] o'erweigh a whole theatre of others. O, there be players that I have seen play,—and heard others praise, and that highly,—not to speak it profanely, that, neither having the accent of Christians,[5] nor the gait of Christian, pagan, nor man, have so strutted and bellow'd, that I have thought some of nature's journeymen had made them, and not made them well, they imitated humanity so abominably.

FIRST PLAYER.

I hope we have reform'd that indifferently[6] with us, sir.

HAMLET.

O, reform it altogether. And let those that play your clowns speak no more than is set down for them: for there be of them that will themselves laugh, to set on some quantity of barren[7] spectators to laugh too; though, in the mean time, some necessary question of the play be then to be consider'd; that's villainous, and shows a most pitiful ambition in the fool that uses it. Go, make you ready.

[*Exeunt* PLAYERS.

Enter POLONIUS, ROSENCRANTZ, *and* GUILDENSTERN.

How now, my lord! will the king hear this piece of work?

POLONIUS.

And the queen too, and that presently.

HAMLET.

Bid the players make haste.   [*Exit* POLONIUS.

---

come tardy off: fall short of an adequate performance. [2] unskilful: indiscriminating. [3] censure: judgment. [4] in your allowance:
your opinion. [5] Christians: the average citizens. [6] reform'd that
indifferently: revised that moderately. [7] barren: stupid.

Will you two help to hasten them?

ROSENCRANTZ *and* GUILDENSTERN.

We will, my lord.

[*Exeunt* ROSENCRANTZ *and* GUILDENSTERN.

HAMLET.

What, ho, Horatio!

Enter HORATIO.

HORATIO.

Here, sweet lord, at your service.

HAMLET.

Horatio, thou art e'en as just[1] a man
As e'er my conversation coped withal.

HORATIO.

O, my dear lord,—

HAMLET.

           Nay, do not think I flatter;
For what advancement[2] may I hope from thee,
That no revenue hast, but thy good spirits,
To feed and clothe thee? Why should the poor be flatter'd?
No, let the candied tongue[3] lick absurd pomp;
And crook the pregnant hinges of the knee[4]
Where thrift[5] may follow fawning. Dost thou hear?
Since my dear soul was mistress of her choice,[6]
And could of men distinguish, her election[7]
Hath seal'd[8] thee for herself: for thou hast been
As one, in suffering all, that suffers nothing;
A man that fortune's buffets and rewards
Hast ta'en with equal thanks: and blest are those
Whose blood[9] and judgement are so well commingled,

---

[1] **just**: well adjusted. [2] **advancement**: reward. [3] **candied tongue**: flatterer. [4] **crook the pregnant hinges of the knee**: bend the ready hinges of the knee. [5] **thrift**: monetary gain. [6] **mistress of her choice**: free. [7] **election**: choice. [8] **seal'd**: reserved. [9] **blood**: temperament.

That they are not a pipe[1] for fortune's finger
To sound what stop she please. Give me that man
That is not passion's slave, and I will wear him
In my heart's core, ay, in my heart of heart,
As I do thee.—Something too much of this.—
There is a play to-night before the king;
One scene of it comes near the circumstance
Which I have told thee of my father's death:
I prithee, when thou seest that act a-foot,
Even with the very comment of thy soul [2]
Observe my uncle: if his occulted guilt[3]
Do not itself unkennel [4] in one speech,
It is a damned ghost that we have seen;
And my imaginations are as foul
As Vulcan's stithy.[5] Give him heedful note:
For I mine eyes will rivet to his face;
And, after, we will both our judgements join
In censure of his seeming.[6]

    HORATIO.

                     Well, my lord:
If he steal aught the whilst this play is playing,
And scape detecting, I will pay the theft.[7]

    HAMLET.

They're coming to the play; I must be idle:[8]
Get you a place.

Danish march. A flourish. Enter KING, QUEEN, POLONIUS,
   OPHELIA, ROSENCRANTZ, GUILDENSTERN, *and other* LORDS
   attendant, with the GUARD *carrying torches.*

    KING.

How fares our cousin Hamlet?

---

[1] pipe: a wind instrument. [2] very comment of they soul: your sharp-
est faculties. [3] occulted guilt: concealed guilt. [4] itself unkennel:
bring out into the open. [5] stithy: blacksmith shop; a smith's forge.
[6] censure of his seeming: judgment of his appearance. [7] If he
steal aught while this play is playing,/An scape detecting;
I will pay the theft: if he should attempt to conceal his emotions,
and get by with it, I shall detect it. [8] be idle: that is, resume his
role of an idiot.

HAMLET.

Excellent, i'faith; of the chameleon's dish:[1] I eat the air, promise-cramm'd: you cannot feed capons so.

KING.

I have nothing with this answer, Hamlet; these words are not mine.[2]

HAMLET.

No, nor mine now.—[to POLONIUS] My lord, you play'd once i'th' university, you say?

POLONIUS.

That did I, my lord; and was accounted[3] a good actor.

HAMLET.

And what did you enact?

POLONIUS.

I did enact Julius Caesar: I was kill'd i'th'Capitol; Brutus kill'd me.

HAMLET.

It was a brute part of him to kill so capital a calf there.—Be the players ready?

ROSENCRANTZ.

Ay, my lord; they stay upon your patience.[4]

QUEEN.

Come hither, my dear Hamlet, sit by me.

HAMLET.

No, good mother; here's metal more attractive.[5]

POLONIUS [to the KING].

O, ho! do you mark that?

HAMLET.

Lady, shall I lie in your lap?

                              [Lying down at OPHELIA's feet.

OPHELIA.

No, my lord.

---

[1] chameleon's dish: chameleons appear to live on air. [2] I have nothing with this answer, Hamlet; these words are not/mine: I do not understand your answer, Hamlet; it has nothing to do with my question. [3] accounted: considered. [4] stay upon your patience: they await your indulgence. [5] metal more attractive: meaning Ophelia.

HAMLET.

I mean, my head upon your lap?

OPHELIA.

Ay, my lord.

HAMLET.

Do you think I meant country[1] matters?

OPHELIA.

I think nothing, my lord.

HAMLET.

That's a fair thought to lie between maids' legs.

OPHELIA.

What is, my lord?

HAMLET.

Nothing.

OPHELIA.

You are merry, my lord.

HAMLET.

Who, I?

OPHELIA.

Ay, my lord.

HAMLET.

O God, your only jig-maker.[2] What should a man do but be merry? For, look you, how cheerfully my mother looks, and my father died within's two hours.

OPHELIA.

Nay, 'tis twice two months, my lord.

HAMLET.

So long? Nay, then, let the devil wear black, for I'll have a suit of sables. O heavens! die two months ago, and not forgotten yet? Then there's hope a great man's memory may outlive his life half a year: but, by'r lady, he must build

---

[1] country: earthy; indelicate.
[2] jig-maker: comic.

churches, then; or else shall he suffer not thinking on,[1] with the hobby-horse,[2] whose epitaph is, 'For, O, for, O, the hobby-horse is forgot.'

Hautboys play. The dumb-show enters.

Enter a KING *and a* QUEEN *very lovingly; the* QUEEN *embracing him, and he her. She kneels, and makes show of protestation unto him. He takes her up, and declines his head upon her neck; lays him down upon a bank of flowers: she, seeing him asleep, leaves him. Anon comes in a fellow, takes off his crown, kisses it, and pours poison in the* KING's *ears, and exit. The* QUEEN *returns; finds the* KING *dead, and makes passionate action. The* POISONER, *with some two or three* MUTES, *comes in again, seeming to lament with her. The dead body is carried away. The* POISONER *wooes the* QUEEN *with gifts: she seems loth and unwilling awhile, but in the end accepts his love.* [*Exeunt.*

OPHELIA.

What means this, my lord?

HAMLET.

Marry, this is miching mallecho;[3] it means mischief

OPHELIA.

Belike[4] this show imports the argument of the play.

Enter PROLOGUE.

HAMLET.

We shall know by this fellow: the players cannot keep counsel;[5] they'll tell all.

OPHELIA.

Will he tell us what this show meant?

---

[1] **suffer not thinking on:** he shall suffer the fate of not being remembered. [2] **hobby-horse:** the May dances in which the hobby-horse appeared were suppressed by the puritanical thought of the times. [3] **miching mallecho:** secret wickedness (Spanish derivation). [4] **Belike:** perhaps. [5] **keep counsel:** keep a secret.

HAMLET.

Ay, or any show that you'll show him: be not you ashamed to
show, he'll not shame to tell you what it means.

OPHELIA.

You are naught,[1] you are naught: I'll mark the play.

PROLOGUE.

> For us, and for our tragedy,
> Here stooping to your clemency,
> We beg your hearing patiently.   [*Exit.*

HAMLET.

Is this a prologue, or the posy[2] of a ring?

OPHELIA.

'Tis brief, my lord.

HAMLET.

As woman's love.

    Enter two PLAYERS, KING *and* QUEEN.

PLAYER KING.

Full thirty times hath Phœbus' cart[3] gone round
Neptune's salt wash[4] and Tellus' orbed ground,[5]
And thirty dozen moons with borrow'd sheen
About the world have times twelve thirties been,
Since love our hearts, and Hymen[6] did our hands,
Unite commutual in most sacred bands.

PLAYER QUEEN.

So many journeys may the sun and moon
Make us again count o'er ere love be done!
But, woe is me, you are sick of late,
So far from cheer and from your former state,
That I distrust you.[7] Yet, though I distrust,
Discomfort you, my lord, it nothing must:[8]
For women's fear and love hold quantity;

---

[1] naught: naughty. [2] posy: poesy; motto or short sentence. [3] Phœbus' cart: the sun god's chariot. [4] Neptune's salt wash: the ocean. [5] Tellus' orbed ground: Tellus was the goddess of the earth. [6] Hymen: god of marriage. [7] I distrust you: I am distrustful on your account. [8] it nothing must: it doesn't matter.

In neither aught, or in extremity.[1]
Now, what my love is, proof hath made you know;
And as my love is sized, my fear is so:
Where love is great, the littlest doubts are fear;
Where little fears grow great, great love grows there.

    PLAYER KING.

Faith, I must leave thee, love, and shortly too;
My operant powers[2] their functions leave to do:
And thou shalt live in this fair world behind,
Honour'd, beloved; and haply one as kind
For husband shalt thou—

    PLAYER QUEEN.

                O, confound the rest!
Such love must needs be treason in my breast:
In second husband let me be accurst!
None wed the second but who kill'd the first.

    HAMLET [aside].

Wormwood, wormwood.

    PLAYER QUEEN.

The instances[3] that second marriage move
Are base respects of thrift,[4] but none of love:
A second time I kill my husband dead
When second husband kisses me in bed.

    PLAYER KING.

I do believe you think what now you speak;
But what we do determine oft we break.
Purpose is but the slave to memory;
Of violent birth, but poor validity:[5]
Which now, like fruit unripe, sticks on the tree;
But fall, unshaken, when they mellow be.
Most necessary 'tis that we forget

---

[1] In neither aught, or in extremity: they go to extremes; there is no middle course.
[2] operant powers: faculties.
[3] instances: considerations.
[4] thrift: wealth.
[5] validity: value.

To pay ourselves what to ourselves is debt:
What to ourselves in passion we propose,
The passion ending, doth the purpose lose.
The violence of either grief or joy
Their own enactures with themselves destroy:
Where joy most revels, grief doth most lament;
Grief joys, joy grieves, on slender accident.[1]
This world is not for aye,[2] nor 'tis not strange
That even our loves should with our fortunes change;
For 'tis a question left us yet to prove,
Whether love lead fortune, or else fortune love.
The great man down, you mark his favourite flies;[3]
The poor advanced makes friends of enemies.
And hitherto doth love on fortune tend:
For who not needs shall never lack a friend;
And who in want a hollow friend doth try,
Directly seasons him his enemy.[4]
But, orderly to end where I begun,—
Our wills and fates do so contrary run,
That our devices[5] still are overthrown;
Our thoughts are ours, their ends none of our own:
So think thou wilt no second husband wed;
But die thy thoughts when thy first lord is dead.

    PLAYER QUEEN.

Nor earth to me give food, nor heaven light!
Sport[6] and repose lock from me day and night!
To desperation turn my trust and hope!
An anchor's cheer[7] in prison be my scope!
Each opposite that blanks the face of joy
Meet what I would have well, and it destroy!
Both here and hence pursue me lasting strife,

---

on slender accident: with the slightest cause. [2] for aye: forever.
[3] favourite flies: his friends leave him. [4] who in want a hollow
friend doth try,/Directly seasons him his enemy: learn the value of
a false friend, go to him when you are in need. [5] devices: plans.
[6] sport: play. [7] anchor's cheer: anchorite's (hermit's) fare.

If, once a widow, ever I be wife!

HAMLET.

If she should break it now!

PLAYER KING.

'Tis deeply sworn. Sweet, leave me here awhile;
My spirits grow dull, and fain I would beguile
The tedious day with sleep.   [Sleep

PLAYER QUEEN.

              Sleep rock thy brain;
And never come mischance between us twain!   [Ex#

HAMLET.

Madam, how like you this play?

QUEEN.

The lady doth protest too much, methinks.

HAMLET.

O, but she'll keep her word.

KING.

Have you heard the argument? [1] Is there no offence in't?

HAMLET.

No, no, they do but jest, poison in jest; no offence i'th'worl

KING.

What do you call the play?

HAMLET.

The Mouse-trap. Marry, how? Tropically. This play is th
image of a murder done in Vienna: Gonzago is the duke'
name; his wife, Baptista: you shall see anon; 'tis a knavish
piece of work: but what o'that? your majesty, and we tha
have free[2] souls, it touches us not: let the gall'd jade wince
our withers are unwrung.[3]

---

[1] argument: plot.
[2] free: innocent of guilt.
[3] let the gall'd jade wince,/our withers are unwrung: let the guilt
cringe; our conscience is clear.

Enter PLAYER, *as* LUCIANUS.

This is one Lucianus, nephew to the king.

OPHELIA.

You are as good as a chorus, my lord.

HAMLET.

I could interpret between you and your love, if I could see the puppets dallying.[1]

OPHELIA.

You are keen, my lord, you are keen.

HAMLET.

It would cost you a groaning to take off my edge.

OPHELIA.

Still better, and worse.

HAMLET.

So you mistake your husbands.—Begin, murderer; pox,[2] leave thy damnable faces, and begin. Come:—the croaking raven doth bellow for revenge.

LUCIANUS.

Thoughts black, hands apt, drugs fit, and time agreeing;
Confederate season, else no creature seeing;
Thou mixture rank, of midnight weeds collected,
With Hecate's[3] ban[4] thrice blasted, thrice infected,
Thy natural magic and dire property,
On wholesome life usurp immediately.

[*Pours the poison in his ears.*

HAMLET.

He poisons him i'th'garden for's estate. His name's Gonzago: the story is extant, and writ in choice Italian: you shall see anon how the murderer gets the love of Gonzago's wife.

OPHELIA.

The king rises.

---

[1] dallying: making love.
[2] pox: a mild oath—a pox on you!
[3] Hecate: a Greek Goddess of witchcraft.
[4] ban: a curse.

HAMLET.

What, frighted with false fire! [1]

QUEEN.

How fares my lord?

POLONIUS.

Give o'er the play.

KING.

Give me some light:—away!

ALL.

Lights, lights, lights.

[*Exeunt all but* HAMLET *and* HORATIO.

HAMLET.

> Why, let the stricken deer go weep,
>> The hart ungalled [2] play;
> For some must watch, while some must sleep:
>> So runs the world away.—

Would not this, sir, and a forest of feathers,[3]—if the rest of my fortunes turn Turk[4] with me,—with two Provincial roses[5] on my razed shoes, get me a fellowship in a cry of players, sir?

HORATIO.

Half a share.

HAMLET.

A whole one, I.

> For thou dost know, O Damon dear,
>> This realm dismantled was
> Of Jove himself; and now reigns here
>> A very, very—pajock.[6]

HORATIO.

You might have rimed.

HAMLET.

O good Horatio, I'll take the ghost's word for a thousand pound. Didst perceive?

---

[1] false fire: blanks.
[2] hart ungalled: uninjured or untroubled male deer.
[3] a forest of feathers: actors' trappings.
[4] Turk: betray.
[5] Provincial roses: rosettes.
[6] pajock: peacock.

HORATIO.

Very well, my lord.

HAMLET.

Upon the talk of the poisoning,—

HORATIO.

I did very well note him.

HAMLET.

Ah, ha!—Come, some music! come, the recorders!—
   For if the king like not the comedy,
   Why, then, belike,[1]—he likes it not, perdy.[2]—
Come, some music!

    Enter ROSENCRANTZ *and* GUILDENSTERN.

GUILDENSTERN.

Good my lord, vouchsafe me a word with you.

HAMLET.

Sir, a whole history.

GUILDENSTERN.

The king, sir,—

HAMLET.

Ay, sir, what of him?

GUILDENSTERN.

Is, in his retirement, marvellous distemper'd.[3]

HAMLET.

With drink, sir?

GUILDENSTERN.

No, my lord, with choler.[4]

HAMLET.

Your wisdom should show itself more richer to signify this to
his doctor; for, for me to put him to his purgation[5] would
perhaps plunge him into far more choler.

---

[1] belike: perhaps.
[2] perdy; *par Dieu* (French oath).
[3] distemper'd: mentally disturbed.
[4] choler: anger.
[5] purgation: act of purging (cleansing); a play on the word.

GUILDENSTERN.

Good my lord, put your discourse into some frame,[1] and star
not so wildly from my affair.

HAMLET.

I am tame, sir:—pronounce.

GUILDENSTERN.

The queen, your mother, in most great affliction of spirit, hath
sent me to you.

HAMLET.

You are welcome.

GUILDENSTERN.

Nay, good my lord, this courtesy is not of the right breed. I
it shall please you to make me a wholesome[2] answer, I will
do your mother's commandment: if not, your pardon and my
return shall be the end of the business.

HAMLET.

Sir, I cannot.

GUILDENSTERN.

What, my lord?

HAMLET.

Make you a wholesome answer; my wit's diseased: but, sir
such answer as I can make, you shall command; or, rather
as you say, my mother: therefore no more, but to the matter:
my mother, you say,—

ROSENCRANTZ.

Then thus she says; your behaviour hath struck her into
amazement and admiration.[3]

HAMLET.

O wonderful son, that can so astonish a mother!—But is there
no sequel at the heels of this mother's admiration? impart.

---

[1] frame: order.
[2] wholesome: reasonable.
[3] amazement and admiration: these words are synonomous here
shock.

ROSENCRANTZ.

She desires to speak with you in her closet,[1] ere you go to bed.

HAMLET.

We shall obey, were she ten times our mother.
Have you any further trade with us?

ROSENCRANTZ.

My lord, you once did love me.

HAMLET.

And do still, by these pickers and stealers.[2]

ROSENCRANTZ.

Good my lord, what is your cause of distemper? you do,
surely, bar the door upon your own liberty, if you deny your
griefs to your friend.

HAMLET.

Sir, I lack advancement.

ROSENCRANTZ.

How can that be, when you have the voice of the king himself[3] for your succession in Denmark?

HAMLET.

Ay, sir, but 'While the grass grows,'[4]—the proverb is something musty.

Enter PLAYERS *with recorders.*

O, the recorders:[5]—let me see one.—To withdraw with you:—
why do you go about to recover the wind of me,[6] as if you
would drive me into a toil?[7]

GUILDENSTERN.

O, my lord, if my duty be too bold, my love is too un-
mannerly.

HAMLET.

I do not well understand that. Will you play upon this pipe?

---

[1] closet: her chambers. [2] pickers and stealers: hands. [3] the voice of
the king him-/self: his promise. [4] "While the grass grows": From
the proverb, "While grass doth growe, the silly horse he starves."
The Paradise of Daintie Devises," 1578. [5] recorders: musical instru-
ments; pipes. [6] recover the wind of me: upwind from me. [7] toil:
trap.

GUILDENSTERN.

My lord, I cannot.

HAMLET.

I pray you.

GUILDENSTERN.

Believe me, I cannot.

HAMLET.

I do beseech you.

GUILDENSTERN.

I know no touch of it, my lord.

HAMLET.

'Tis as easy as lying: govern these ventages[1] with your finge
and thumb, give it breath with your mouth, and it will dis
course most eloquent music. Look you, these are the stops.

GUILDENSTERN.

But these cannot I command to any utterance of harmony;
have not the skill.

HAMLET.

Why, look you now, how unworthy a thing you make of me
You would play upon me; you would seem to know my
stops; you would pluck out the heart of my mystery;[2] yo
would sound me from my lowest note to the top of my com
pass: and there is much music, excellent voice, in this littl
organ; yet cannot you make it speak. 'Sblood, do you think
am easier to be play'd on than a pipe? Call me what instru
ment you will, though you can fret[3] me, you cannot pla
upon me.

Enter POLONIUS.

God bless you, sir!

POLONIUS.

My lord, the queen would speak with you, and presently.

---

[1] ventages: openings.
[2] mystery: secret.
[3] fret: pluck at.

HAMLET.

Do you see yonder cloud that's almost in shape of a camel?

POLONIUS.

By th'mass, and 'tis like a camel, indeed.

HAMLET.

Methinks it is like a weasel.

POLONIUS.

It is backt like a weasel.

HAMLET.

Or like a whale?

POLONIUS.

Very like a whale.

HAMLET.

Then will I come to my mother by and by.—They fool me to the top of my bent.[1]—I will come by and by.

POLONIUS.

I will say so.

HAMLET.

By and by is easily said.   [*Exit* POLONIUS.]—
Leave me, friends.

[*Exeunt* ROSENCRANTZ GUILDENSTERN, HORATIO, *and* PLAYERS.
'Tis now the very witching time of night,
When churchyards yawn, and hell itself breathes out
Contagion to this world: now could I drink hot blood,
And do such bitter business as the day
Would quake to look on. Soft! now to my mother.—
heart, lose not thy nature; let not ever

They fool me to the top of my bent: they force me to play my masquerade to the limit of my ability.

The soul of Nero[1] enter this firm bosom:
Let me be cruel, not unnatural:[2]
I will speak daggers to her, but use none;
My tongue and soul in this be hypocrites,—
How in my words soever she be shent,[3]
To give them seals[4] never, my soul, consent!   [*Exit.*

SCENE III.

A room in the castle.

Enter KING, ROSENCRANTZ, *and* GUILDENSTERN.

KING.

I like him not; nor stands it safe with us
To let his madness range. Therefore prepare you;
I your commission will forthwith dispatch,[5]
And he to England shall along with you:
The terms of our estate[6] may not endure
Hazard so dangerous as doth hourly grow
Out of his lunacies.

GUILDENSTERN.

We will ourselves provide:
Most holy and religious fear it is
To keep those many many bodies safe
That live and feed upon your majesty.

ROSENCRANTZ.

The single and peculiar[7] life is bound,
With all the strength and armour of the mind,
To keep itself from noyance,[8] but much more
That spirit upon whose weal [9] depends and rests
The lives of many. The cease of majesty

---

[1] Nero: Roman Emperor, murdered his mother, Agrippina. [2] unnatural: murderous. [3] be shent: be dishonored. [4] seals: to put them in execution. [5] dispatch: draw up. [6] terms of our estate: stability of our government. [7] peculiar: exclusive. [8] noyance: harmful distraction. [9] weal: welfare.

Dies not alone; but, like a gulf,[1] doth draw
What's near it with it: 'tis a massy[2] wheel,
Fixt on the summit of the highest mount,
To whose huge spokes ten thousand lesser things
Are mortised and adjoin'd; which, when it falls, .
Each small annexment, petty consequence,
Attends the boisterous[3] ruin. Ne'er alone
Did the king sigh, but with a general groan.

    KING.

Arm you,[4] I pray you, to this speedy voyage;
For we will fetters put upon this fear,
Which now goes too free-footed.

    ROSENCRANTZ *and* GUILDENSTERN.

                We will haste us.

        [*Exeunt* ROSENCRANTZ *and* GUILDENSTERN.

        Enter POLONIUS

    POLONIUS.

My lord, he's going to his mother's closet:
Behind the arras[5] I'll convey[6] myself,
To hear the process; I'll warrant she'll tax him home:[7]
And, as you said, and wisely was it said,
'Tis meet that some more audience than a mother,
Since nature makes them partial, should o'erhear
The speech, of vantage.[8] Fare you well, my liege:
I'll call upon you ere you go to bed,
And tell you what I know.

    KING.

            Thanks, dear my lord.

               [*Exit* POLONIUS.

O, my offence is rank, it smells to heaven;
It hath the primal eldest curse[9] upon't,—

---

[1] **gulf:** vortex. [2] **massy:** massive. [3] **boisterous:** massive; cumbrous.
[4] **arm you:** prepare yourself. [5] **arras:** drapery. [6] **convey:** hide. [7] **tax him home:** thoroughly take him to task. [8] **of vantage:** from an advantageous spot. [9] **primal eldest curse:** the mark of Cain.

A brother's murder!—Pray can I not,
Though inclination be as sharp as will:
My stronger guilt defeats my strong intent;
And, like a man to double business bound,
I stand in pause where I shall first begin,
And both neglect. What if this cursed hand
Were thicker than itself with brother's blood,
Is there not rain enough in the sweet heavens
To wash it white as snow? Whereto serves mercy
But to confront the visage of offence? [1]
And what's in prayer[2] but this twofold force,—
To be forestalled ere we come to fall,
Or pardon'd being down? Then I'll look up;
My fault is past. But, O, what form of prayer
Can serve my turn? 'Forgive me my foul murder'?—
That cannot be; since I am still possest
Of those effects[3] for which I did the murder,—
My crown, mine own ambition, and my queen.
May one be pardon'd, and retain th'offence? [4]
In the corrupted currents of this world
Offence's gilded hand may shove by justice;
And oft 'tis seen the wicked prize itself
Buys out the law: but 'tis not so above;
There is no shuffling,—there the action lies
In his true nature; and we ourselves compell'd,
Even to the teeth and forehead[5] of our faults,
To give in evidence. What then? what rests? [6]
Try what repentance can: what can it not?
Yet what can it when one can not repent?
O wretched state! O bosom black as death!
O limed[7] soul, that, struggling to be free,
Art more engaged! Help, angels! Make assay:[8]

---

[1] Whereto serves mercy/But to confront the visage of offence:
mercy is the only defender of the guilty. [2] prayer: the Lord's
Prayer. [3] effects: possessions. [4] offence: gains of sin. [5] teeth and
forehead: to the limit. [6] what rests: what remains. [7] limed: bird-
lime was a sticky substance used to snare birds. [8] Make assay: test
me.

ow, stubborn knees; and, heart with strings of steel,
e soft as sinews of the new-born babe!
ll may be well.   *[Retires and kneels.*

Enter HAMLET.

HAMLET.

Now might I do it pat,[1] now he is praying;
And now I'll do't:—and so he goes to heaven;
And so am I revenged:—that would be scann'd:[2]
A villain kills my father; and, for that,
, his sole son, do this same villain send
To heaven.

O, this is hire and salary, not revenge.
He took my father grossly, full of bread;[3]
With all his crimes broad blown,[4] as flush as May;[5]
And how his audit[6] stands who knows save heaven?
But, in our circumstance and course of thought,
'Tis heavy with him: and am I, then, revenged,
To take him in the purging of his soul,
When he is fit and season'd for his passage?
No.

Up, sword; and know thou a more horrid hent:[7]
When he is drunk, asleep, or in his rage;
Or in th'incestuous pleasure of his bed;
At gaming, swearing; or about some act
That has no relish[8] of salvation in't;—
Then trip him, that his heels may kick at heaven;
And that his soul may be as damn'd and black
As hell, whereto it goes. My mother stays:
This physic[9] but prolongs thy sickly days.   *[Exit.*

KING [*rising*].

My words fly up, my thoughts remain below:

---

do it pat: do it suitably. [2] scann'd: examined. [3] grossly, **full of
bread**: enjoying the pleasures of this world. [4] **broad blown**: broad-
cast to the public. [5] **flush as May**: the vigorous time of life. [6] **audit**:
record. [7] **horrid hent**: deadly opportunity. [8] **relish**: meaning. [9] **physic:**
remedy.

SCENE IV.

The Queen's closet.

Enter QUEEN *and* POLONIUS.

POLONIUS.

He will come straight.[1] Look you lay home to him:
Tell him his pranks have been too broad [2] to bear with,
And that your Grace hath screen'd and stood between
Much heat and him. I'll sconce me[3] even here.
Pray you, be round [4] with him.

HAMLET [*within*].

Mother, mother, mother!

QUEEN.

I'll warrant[5] you; fear me not:—withdraw,
I hear him coming.   [POLONIUS *goes behind the arras.*

Enter HAMLET.

HAMLET.

Now, mother, what's the matter?

QUEEN.

Hamlet, thou hast thy father much offended.

HAMLET.

Mother, you have my father much offended.

QUEEN.

Come, come, you answer with an idle tongue.

HAMLET.

Go, go, you question with a wicked tongue.

---

[1] straight: immediately.
[2] broad: unrestrained.
[3] sconce me: conceal myself.
[4] round: blunt.
[5] warrant: protect.

QUEEN.

Why, how now, Hamlet!

HAMLET.

What's the matter now?

QUEEN.

Have you forgot me?

HAMLET.

No, by the rood,[1] not so:

You are the queen, your husband's brother's wife;

And—would it were not so!—you are my mother.

QUEEN.

Nay, then, I'll set those to you that can speak.

HAMLET.

Come, come, and sit you down; you shall not budge;

You go not till I set you up a glass[2]

Where you may see the inmost part of you.

QUEEN.

What wilt thou do? thou wilt not murder me?—

Help, help, ho!

POLONIUS [behind].

What, ho! help, help, help!

HAMLET [drawing].

How now! a rat? Dead for a ducat,[3] dead!

[Makes a pass through the arras.

POLONIUS [behind].

O, I am slain!   [Falls and dies.

QUEEN.

O me, what hast thou done?

HAMLET.

Nay, I know not: is it the king?

QUEEN.

O, what a rash and bloody deed is this!

---

[1] rood: the crucifix.
[2] glass: mirror.
[3] ducat: a gold coin.

HAMLET.

A bloody deed!—almost as bad, good mother,
As kill a king, and marry with his brother.

QUEEN.

As kill a king!

HAMLET.

        Ay, lady 'twas my word.—

             [Lifts up the arras, and sees POLONIUS

Thou wretched, rash, intruding fool, farewell!
I took thee for thy better:[1] take thy fortune;
Thou find'st to be too busy is some danger.—
Leave wringing of your hands: peace; sit you down,
And let me wring your heart: for so I shall,
If it be made of penetrable stuff;
If damned custom[2] have not brazed[3] it so,
That it is proof and bulwark against sense.[4]

QUEEN.

What have I done, that thou darest wag thy tongue
In noise so rude against me?

HAMLET.

               Such an act
That blurs the grace and blush of modesty;
Calls virtue hypocrite; takes off the rose
From the fair forehead of an innocent love,
And sets a blister[5] there; makes marriage-vows
As false as dicers' oaths:[6] O, such a deed
As from the body of contraction[7] plucks
The very soul; and sweet religion makes
A rhapsody of words: heaven's face doth glow;
Yea, this solidity and compound mass,
With tristful[8] visage, as against the doom,
Is thought-sick at the act.

---

[1] **thy better:** the king. [2] **custom:** habit. [3] **brazed:** hardened. [4] **proof and bulwark against sense:** protection against feeling. [5] **a blister:** brand of a harlot. [6] **dicers' oaths:** gamblers' promises. [7] **contraction:** marriage contract. [8] **tristful:** melancholy.

QUEEN.

                    Ay me, what act,
That roars so loud, and thunders in the index? [1]

HAMLET.

Look here, upon this picture and on this,
The counterfeit presentment[2] of two brothers.
See, what a grace was seated on this brow;
Hyperion's[3] curls; the front of Jove himself;[4]
An eye like Mars,[5] to threaten and command;
A station[6] like the herald Mercury[7]
New-lighted on a heaven-kissing hill;
A combination and a form indeed,
Where every god did seem to set his seal,
To give the world assurance of a man:
This was your husband.—Look you now, what follows:
Here is your husband; like a mildew'd ear,
Blasting his wholesome brother. Have you eyes?
Could you on this fair mountain[8] leave to feed,
And batten on this moor? [9] Ha! have you eyes?
You cannot call it love; for at your age
The hey-day in the blood is tame, it's humble,
And waits upon the judgement: and what judgement
Would step from this to this? Sense, sure, you have,
Else could you not have motion: but, sure, that sense
Is apoplext:[10] for madness would not err;
Nor sense to ecstasy was ne'er so thrall'd [11]
But it reserved some quantity of choice,
To serve in such a difference. What devil was't
That thus hath cozen'd [12] you to hoodman-blind? [13]
Eyes without feeling, feeling without sight,

---

index: prelude. [2] counterfeit presentment: pictured. [3] Hyperion:
identified with Apollo, god of manly beauty. [4] the front of Jove
himself: the face of Jove, chief Roman god. [5] Mars: god of war.
[6] station: stance. [7] the herald Mercury: the messenger of the Roman
gods. [8] fair mountain: the murdered King Hamlet. [9] moor: poor,
unproductive land (King Claudius). [10] apoplext: paralyzed.
[11] thrall'd: enslaved. [12] cozen'd: cheated. [13] hoodman-blind: blind-
man's buff.

Ears without hands or eyes, smelling sans[1] all,
Or but a sickly part of one true sense
Could not so mope.[2]
O shame! where is thy blush? Rebellious hell,
If thou canst mutine in a matron's bones,
To flaming youth let virtue be as wax,
And melt in her own fire: proclaim no shame
When the compulsive ardour gives the charge,[3]
Since frost itself as actively doth burn,
And reason pandars will:[4]

QUEEN.

     O Hamlet, speak no more:
Thou turn'st mine eyes into my very soul;
And there I see such black and grained[5] spots
As will not leave their tinct.[6]

HAMLET.

     Nay, but to live
In the rank sweat of an enseamed[7] bed,
Stew'd in corruption, honeying and making love
Over the nasty sty,—

QUEEN.

    O, speak to me no more;
These words, like daggers, enter in mine ears;
No more, sweet Hamlet!

HAMLET.

    A murderer and a villain;
A slave that is not twentieth part the tithe
Of your precedent lord; a vice[8] of kings;
A cutpurse[9] of the empire and the rule,
That from a shelf the precious diadem stole,
And put it in his pocket!

QUEEN.

     No more!

---

[1] sans: without. [2] mope: be bewildered. [3] gives the charge: attacks
[4] reason pandars will: reason paves the way for desire. [5] grained
indelibly dyed. [6] tinct: color. [7] enseamed: greasy. [8] vice: a clown
ish buffoon in a morality play, representing one of the vices. [9] cut
purse: thief.

HAMLET.

A king of shreds and patches,—

Enter GHOST.

Save me, and hover o'er me with your wings,
You heavenly guards!—What would your gracious figure?

QUEEN.

Alas, he's mad!

HAMLET.

Do you not come your tardy son to chide,
That, lapsed in time and passion,[1] lets go by
Th'important[2] acting of your dread command?
O, say!

GHOST.

Do not forget: this visitation
Is but to whet thy almost blunted purpose.
But, look, amazement on thy mother sits:
O, step between her and her fighting soul,—
Conceit[3] in weakest bodies strongest works,—
Speak to her, Hamlet.

HAMLET.

                    How is it with you, lady?

QUEEN.

Alas, how is't with you,
That you do bend your eye on vacancy,
And with th'incorporal[4] air do hold discourse?
Forth at your eyes your spirits wildly peep;
And, as the sleeping soldiers in th'alarm,
Your bedded[5] hair, like life in excrements,[6]
Start up, and stand an end.[7] O gentle son,
Upon the heat and flame of thy distemper
Sprinkle cool patience. Whereon do you look?

---

[1] **lapsed in time and passion:** having suffered time to pass and passion to cool. [2] **important:** urgent. [3] **conceit:** imagination. [4] **incorporal:** bodiless; immaterial. [5] **bedded:** matted. [6] **excrements:** outgrowths, such as nails or hair. [7] **an end:** on end.

HAMLET.

On him, on him! Look you, how pale he glares!
His form and cause conjoin'd,[1] preaching to stones,
Would make them capable.[2]—Do not look upon me;
Lest with this piteous action you convert
My stern effects:[3] then what I have to do
Will want true colour;[4] tears perchance for blood.

QUEEN.

To whom do you speak this?

HAMLET.

Do you see nothing there?

QUEEN.

Nothing at all; yet all that is I see.

HAMLET.

Nor did you nothing hear?

QUEEN.

No, nothing but ourselves.

HAMLET.

Why, look you there! look, how it steals away!
My father, in his habit as he lived!
Look, where he goes, even now, out at the portal!

[*Exit* GHOST.

QUEEN.

This is the very coinage[5] of your brain:
This bodiless creation ecstasy
Is very cunning in.[6]

HAMLET.

Ecstasy!

My pulse, as yours, doth temperately keep time,
And makes as healthful music:[7] it is not madness
That I have utter'd: bring me to the test,
And I the matter will re-word; which madness
Would gambol[8] from. Mother, for love of grace,
Lay not that flattering unction[9] to your soul,

---

[1] **conjoined**: joined together. [2] **capable**: susceptible. [3] **you convert/
My stern effects**: you turn me away from my steady resolution.
[4] **want true colour**: lack its proper character. [5] **coinage**: imagin-
ings. [6] **bodiless creation ecstasy/Is very cunning in**: madness is
very good at imagining these bodiless creations or ghosts. [7] **healthful music**: normal beat. [8] **gambol**: spring away. [9] **flattering unction**:
deceptive forgiveness.

That not your trespass, but my madness speaks:
It will but skin and film the ulcerous place,
Whilst rank corruption, mining all within,
Infects unseen. Confess yourself to heaven;
Repent what's past; avoid what is to come;
And do not spread the compost on the weeds,[1]
To make them ranker. Forgive me this my virtue;
For in the fatness of these pursy[2] times
Virtue itself of vice must pardon beg,
Yea, curb[3] and woo for leave to do him good.

    QUEEN.

O Hamlet, thou hast cleft my heart in twain.

    HAMLET.

O, throw away the worser part of it,
And live the purer with the other half.
Good night: but go not to my uncle's bed;
Assume a virtue, if you have it not.
That monster, custom, who all sense doth eat,
Of habits devil,[4] is angel yet in this,
That to the use of actions fair and good
He likewise gives a frock or livery,
That aptly is put on. Refrain to-night;
And that shall lend a kind of easiness
To the next abstinence: the next more easy;
For use almost can change the stamp of nature,
And either master the devil, or throw him out
With wondrous potency. Once more, good night:
And when you are desirous to be blest,
I'll blessing beg of you.—For this same lord,

                      [*Pointing to* POLONIUS.

I do repent: but heaven hath pleased it so,
To punish me with this, and this with me,
That I must be their scourge and minister.

---

[1] do not spread the compost on the weeds: do not, by new in-
dulgences, heighten your former sins.
[2] pursy: ill-conditioned.
[3] curb: truckle to.
[4] habits devil: devilish habits.

I will bestow him, and will answer well
The death I gave him. So, again, good night.—
I must be cruel, only to be kind:
Thus bad begins, and worse remains behind.[1]—
One word more, good lady.

QUEEN.

What shall I do?

HAMLET.

Not this, by no means, that I bid you do:
Let the bloat[2] king tempt you again to bed;
Pinch wanton on your cheek; call you his mouse;
And let him, for a pair of reechy[3] kisses,
Or paddling in your neck with his damn'd fingers,
Make you to ravel [4] all this matter out,
That I essentially am not in madness,
But mad in craft.[5] 'Twere good you let him know;
For who, that's but a queen, fair, sober, wise,
Would from a paddock,[6] from a bat, a gib,[7]
Such dear concernings[8] hide? who would do so?
No, in despite of sense and secrecy,
Unpeg[9] the basket on the house's top,
Let the birds fly, and, like the famous ape,
To try conclusions,[10] in the basket creep,
And break your own neck down.

QUEEN.

Be thou assured, if words be made of breath
And breath of life, I have no life to breathe
What thou hast said to me.

HAMLET.

I must to England; you know that?

QUEEN.

Alack,
I had forgot: 'tis so concluded on.[11]

---

[1] worse remains behind: the worst is to follow. [2] bloat: bloated;
[3] reechy: reeking; sweaty. [4] to ravel: disclose. [5] craft: cunning.
[6] paddock: toad. [7] gib: cat. [8] dear concernings: matters that are of
so much concern to him. [9] Unpeg: unfasten. [10] conclusions: ex-
periments. [11] concluded on: decided.

HAMLET.

There's letters seal'd: and my two school-fellows,—
Whom I will trust as I will adders fang'd,[1]—
They bear the mandate; they must sweep my way,
And marshal me to knavery. Let it work;
For 'tis the sport to have the enginer
Hoist with his own petar:[2] and 't shall go hard
But I will delve[3] one yard below their mines,
And blow them at the moon: O, 'tis most sweet
When in one line two crafts directly meet.[4]—
This man shall set me packing:
I'll lug the guts[5] into the neighbour[6] room.—
Mother, good night.—Indeed, this counsellor
Is now most still, most secret, and most grave,
Who was in life a foolish prating knave.
Come, sir, to draw toward an end with you.—
Good night, mother.

        [*Exeunt severally;* HAMLET *tugging in* POLONIUS.

---

[1] adders fang'd: snakes with fans undrawn.
[2] petar: petard.
[3] delve: dig.
[4] two crafts directly meet: two enemy plans meet head-on.
[5] guts: the body.
[6] neighbour: adjoining.

Hamlet

ACT 4

ACT IV

CLAUDIUS, realizing that Hamlet will attempt to kill him, sends the Prince to England with Rosencrantz and Guildenstern, who carry a letter asking for Hamlet's death. On the way to the ship Hamlet meets a captain of Fortinbras' army, passing through Denmark with safe-conduct on its way to battle. He broods about the disparity between this young man of action and himself. Ophelia, deeply grieved by her father's death, has gone mad, and her brother, who has heard of the killing of Polonius, has returned to Denmark intent upon vengeance. He forces his way into the castle, but Claudius calms him and promises to give him satisfaction. In the meantime, Horatio has received a letter from Hamlet, telling him that he has been taken by pirates and ransomed back. Claudius and Laertes, also informed that Hamlet is in Denmark, plot his death by devising a fencing match in which Laertes will use a poisoned rapier. To make doubly certain Claudius will have a poisoned drink on hand. At this moment Gertrude enters to tell them of the drowning of Ophelia.

ACT IV. Scene I.

A room in the castle.

Enter KING, QUEEN, ROSENCRANTZ, *and* GUILDENSTERN.

KING.
There's matter[1] in these sighs, these profound heaves:
You must translate: 'tis fit we understand them.
Where is your son?

QUEEN.
Bestow this place on us[2] a little while.
                [*Exeunt* ROSENCRANTZ *and* GUILDENSTERN.
Ah, my good lord, what have I seen to-night!

KING.
What, Gertrude? How does Hamlet?

---

[1] matter: meaning.
[2] Bestow this place on us: leave us alone.

QUEEN.

Mad as the sea and wind, when both contend
Which is the mightier: in his lawless[1] fit,
Behind the arras hearing something stir,
Whips out his rapier, cries 'A rat, a rat!'
And, in this brainish apprehension,[2] kills
The unseen good old man.

KING.

                O heavy deed!

It had been so with us, had we been there:
His liberty is full of threats to all;
To you yourself, to us, to every one.
Alas, how shall this bloody deed be answer'd?
It will be laid to us, whose providence
Should have kept short,[3] restrain'd, and out of haunt[4]
This mad young man: but so much was our love,
We would not understand what was most fit;
But, like the owner of a foul disease,
To keep it from divulging, let it feed
Even on the pith[5] of life. Where is he gone?

QUEEN.

To draw apart the body he hath kill'd:
O'er whom his very madness, like some ore[6]
Among a mineral of metals base,
Shows itself pure; he weeps for what is done.

KING.

O Gertrude, come away!
The sun no sooner shall the mountains touch,

---

[1] lawless: ungovernable.
[2] brainish apprehension: brain-sick mood.
[3] short: tethered; under control.
[4] out of haunt: out of company; away from other people.
[5] pith: essence.
[6] some ore: a vein of precious metal.

But we will ship him hence: and this vile deed
We must, with all our majesty and skill,
Both countenance[1] and excuse.—Ho, Guildenstern!

      Enter ROSENCRANTZ *and* GUILDENSTERN.

Friends both, go join you with some further aid:
Hamlet in madness hath Polonius slain,
And from his mother's closet hath he draggg'd him:
Go seek him out; speak fair,[2] and bring the body
Into the chapel. I pray you, haste in this.

        [*Exeunt* ROSENCRANTZ *and* GUILDENSTERN.

Come, Gertrude, we'll call up our wisest friends;
And let them know both what we mean to do,
And what's untimely done: so, haply,[3] slander—
Whose whisper o'er the world's diameter,
As level[4] as the cannon to his blank,[5]
Transports his poison'd shot—may miss our name,
And hit the woundless[6] air.—O, come away!
My soul is full of discord and dismay.   [*Exeunt.*

SCENE II.

Another room in the castle.

Enter HAMLET.

HAMLET.
Safely stow'd.

ROSENCRANTZ *and* GUILDENSTERN [*within*].
Hamlet! Lord Hamlet!

HAMLET.
What noise? Who calls on Hamlet? O, here they come.

---

[1] **countenance:** sanction.
[2] **fair:** in a friendly manner.
[3] **haply:** by chance.
[4] **level:** well aimed.
[5] **blank:** target; the white mark at which shot or arrows were aimed.
[6] **woundless:** invulnerable.

Enter ROSENCRANTZ *and* GUILDENSTERN.

ROSENCRANTZ.

What have you done, my lord, with the dead body?

HAMLET.

Compounded it with dust, whereto 'tis kin.

ROSENCRANTZ.

Tell us where 'tis; that we may take it thence,
And bear it to the chapel.

HAMLET.

Do not believe it.

ROSENCRANTZ.

Believe what?

HAMLET.

That I can keep your counsel, and not mine own.
Besides, to be demanded of a sponge!—what replication[1]
should be made by the son of a king?

ROSENCRANTZ.

Take you me for a sponge, my lord?

HAMLET.

Ay, sir; that soaks up the king's countenance,[2] his rewards, his
authorities. But such officers do the king best service in the
end: he keeps them, like an ape, in the corner of his jaw;
first mouth'd, to be last swallow'd: when he needs what you
have glean'd, it is but squeezing you, and, sponge, you shall
be dry again.

ROSENCRANTZ.

I understand you not, my lord.

HAMLET.

I am glad of it: a knavish speech sleeps in a foolish ear.

---

[1] replication: plea or answer to a charge.
[2] countenance: favor.

ROSENCRANTZ.

My lord, you must tell us where the body is, and go with us
to the king.

HAMLET.

The body is with the king, but the king is not with the body.
The king is a thing—

GUILDENSTERN.

A thing, my lord?

HAMLET.

Of nothing: bring me to him. Hide fox, and all after.[1]

[*Exeunt.*

SCENE III.

Another room in the castle.

Enter KING, *attended.*

KING.

I have sent to seek him, and find the body.
How dangerous is it that this man goes loose!
Yet must not we put the strong law[2] on him:
He's loved of the distracted [3] multitude,
Who like not in their judgement, but their eyes;
And where 'tis so, th'offender's scourge[4] is weigh'd,
But never the offence. To bear all smooth and even,
This sudden sending him away must seem
Deliberate pause:[5] diseases desperate grown
By desperate appliance are relieved,[6]
Or not at all.

Enter ROSENCRANTZ.

How now! what hath befaln?

ROSENCRANTZ.

Where the dead body is bestow'd, my lord,
We cannot get from him.

---

[1] Hide fox, and all after: a game. [2] the strong law: accuse of a
capital offense. [3] Distracted: confused. [4] scourge: punishment. [5] Deliberate pause: a planned delay. [6] diseases desperate grown/By
desperate appliance are relieved: desperate situations call for desperate measures.

KING.

> But where is he?

ROSENCRANTZ.

Without, my lord; guarded, to know your pleasure.

KING.

Bring him before us.

ROSENCRANTZ.

Ho, Guildenstern! bring in my lord.

> *Enter* HAMLET *and* GUILDENSTERN.

KING.

Now, Hamlet, where's Polonius?

HAMLET.

At supper.

KING.

At supper! where?

HAMLET.

Not where he eats, but where he is eaten: a certain convocation of politic worms are e'en at him.[1] Your worm is your only emperor for diet: we fat all creatures else to fat us, and we fat ourselves for maggots: your fat king and your lean beggar is but variable service,—two dishes, but to one table: that's the end.

KING.

Alas, alas!

HAMLET.

A man may fish with the worm that hath eat of a king, and eat of the fish that hath fed of that worm.

KING.

What dost thou mean by this?

---

[1] a certain convoca-/tion of politic worms are e'en at him: an allusion to the Diets of the Empire at Worms.

HAMLET.

Nothing but to show you how a king may go a progress[1]
through the guts of a beggar.

KING.

Where is Polonius?

HAMLET.

In heaven; send thither to see: if your messenger find him not
there, seek him i'th'other place yourself. But, indeed, if you
find him not within this month, you shall nose him as you go
up the stairs into the lobby.

KING.

Go seek him there.   [*To some* ATTENDANTS.

HAMLET.

He will stay till ye come.   [*Exeunt* ATTENDANTS.

KING.

Hamlet, this deed, for thine especial safety,—
Which we do tender,[2] as we dearly grieve
For that which thou hast done,—must send thee hence
With fiery quickness: therefore prepare thyself;
The bark[3] is ready, and the wind at help,[4]
Th'associates tend, and every thing is bent[5]
For England.

HAMLET.

      For England!

KING.

                  Ay, Hamlet.

HAMLET.

                            Good.

KING.

So is it, if thou knew'st our purposes.

HAMLET.

I see a cherub[6] that sees them.—But, come; for England!—

---

[1] **progress:** royal journey of state. [2] **tender:** have regard for. [3] **bark:**
ship. [4] **at help:** favorable. [5] **bent:** aimed. [6] **cherub:** cherubs are
angels of love; they, therefore, know of such true affection as the
King's for Hamlet (sarcasm).

Farewell, dear mother.

    KING.

Thy loving father, Hamlet.

    HAMLET.

My mother: father and mother is man and wife; man and
wife is one flesh; and so, my mother.—Come, for England!

                                         [*Exit.*

    KING.

Follow him at foot; tempt him with speed aboard;
Delay it not; I'll have him hence to-night:
Away! for every thing is seal'd and done
That else leans[1] on th'affair: pray you, make haste.

                [*Exeunt* ROSENCRANTZ *and* GUILDENSTERN.

And, England, if my love thou hold'st at aught,[2]—
As my great power thereof may give thee sense,[3]
Since yet thy cicatrice[4] looks raw and red
After the Danish sword, and thy free awe[5]
Pays homage to us,—thou mayst not coldly set[6]
Our sovereign process; which imports at full,[7]
By letters conjuring to that effect,
The present[8] death of Hamlet. Do it, England;
For like the hectic[9] in my blood he rages,
And thou must cure me: till I know 'tis done,
Howe'er my haps,[10] my joys were ne'er begun.   [*Exit*

SCENE IV.

A plain in Denmark.

Enter FORTINBRAS *with his* ARMY *over the stage.*

    FORTINBRAS.

Go, captain, from me greet the Danish king;
Tell him that, by his license, Fortinbras
Claims the conveyance[11] of a promised march

---

[1] leans: depends. [2] at aught: of any value. [3] great power thereof
may give thee sense: make them realize this power. [4] cicatrice:
a scar from a wound. [5] free awe: awe still felt, though not enforced
by the presence of the Danish army in England. [6] set: set at
naught. [7] imports at full: urges earnestly. [8] present: immediate.
[9] hectic: fever. [10] Howe'er my haps: however my fortune turns.
[11] conveyance: escort.

Over his kingdom. You know the rendezvous.
If that his majesty would aught with us,
We shall express our duty in his eye;[1]
And let him know so.

    CAPTAIN.

                    I will do't, my lord.

    FORTINBRAS.

Go softly on.   [*Exeunt all but* CAPTAIN.

  Enter HAMLET, ROSENCRANTZ, GUILDENSTERN, *and others.*

    HAMLET.

Good sir, whose powers[2] are these?

    CAPTAIN.

They are of Norway, sir.

    HAMLET.

How purposed, sir, I pray you?

    CAPTAIN.

Against some part of Poland.

    HAMLET.

Who commands them, sir?

    CAPTAIN.

The nephew to old Norway, Fortinbras.

    HAMLET.

Goes it against the main of Poland,[3] sir,
Or for some frontier?

    CAPTAIN.

Truly to speak, sir, and with no addition,
We go to gain a little patch of ground
That hath in it no profit but the name.
To pay five ducats, five, I would not farm it;
Nor will it yield to Norway or the Pole
A ranker[4] rate, should it be sold in fee.[5]

---

[1] eye: presence.
[2] powers: army.
[3] main of Poland: the main force of Poland.
[4] ranker: higher.
[5] in fee: outright.

HAMLET.

Why, then, the Polack never will defend it.

CAPTAIN.

Yes, it is already garrison'd.

HAMLET.

Two thousand souls and twenty thousand ducats
Will not debate the question of this straw:[1]
This is th'imposthume[2] of much wealth and peace,
That inward breaks, and shows no cause without
Why the man dies.—I humbly thank you, sir.

CAPTAIN.

God be wi' you, sir.   [*Exit.*

ROSENCRANTZ.

     Will't please you go, my lord?

HAMLET.

I'll be with you straight. Go a little before.

       [*Exeunt all but* HAMLET

How all occasions do inform against me,
And spur my dull [3] revenge! What is a man,
If his chief good and market of his time[4]
Be but to sleep and feed? a beast, no more.
Sure, he that made us with such large discourse,[5]
Looking before and after, gave us not
That capability and godlike reason
To fust[6] in us unused. Now, whether it be
Bestial oblivion, or some craven scruple[7]
Of thinking too precisely on th'event,—
A thought which, quarter'd, hath but one part wisdom
And ever three parts coward,—I do not know
Why yet I live to say 'This thing's to do;'
Sith[8] I have cause, and will, and strength, and means
To do't. Examples, gross[9] as earth, exhort me:

---

[1] debate the question of this straw: settle the argument by drawing straws. [2] imposthume: internal infection. [3] dull: slow. [4] market of his time: the business in which he employs his time. [5] large discourse: great understanding. [6] fust: molder. [7] craven scruple: cowardly hesitation. [8] Sith: since. [9] gross: plain, or obvious.

Witness this army, of such mass and charge,[1]
Led by a delicate and tender prince;
Whose spirit, with divine ambition puft,
Makes mouths at[2] the invisible event;
Exposing what is mortal and unsure
To all that fortune, death, and danger dare,
Even for an egg-shell. Rightly to be great
Is not to stir without great argument,[3]
But greatly to find quarrel in a straw[4]
When honour's at the stake. How stand I, then,
That have a father kill'd, a mother stain'd,
Excitements of my reason and my blood,
And let all sleep? while, to my shame, I see
The imminent death of twenty thousand men,
That for a fantasy and trick of fame[5]
Go to their graves like beds,[6] fight for a plot
Whereon the numbers cannot try the cause,
Which is not tomb enough and continent[7]
To hide the slain?—O, from this time forth,
My thoughts be bloody,[8] or be nothing worth!   [*Exit.*

SCENE V.
Elsinore. A room in the castle.
Enter QUEEN *and* HORATIO.

QUEEN.
I will not speak with her.
HORATIO.
She is importunate, indeed distract;[9]
Her mood will needs be pitied.
QUEEN.
What would she have?
HORATIO.
She speaks much of her father; says she hears

---

mass and charge: size and importance. [2] Makes mouths at:
ridicules. [3] argument: cause. [4] in a straw: at a trifle. [5] a fantasy
and trick of fame: an illusion and a whim that promise fame.
[6] like beds: as to their beds. [7] continent: capacious enough.
[8] bloody: violent. [9] distract: distraught.

There's tricks i'th'world;[1] and hems, and beats her heart;
Spurns enviously at straws;[2] speaks things in doubt,
That carry but half sense: her speech is nothing,
Yet the unshaped use of it doth move
The hearers to collection;[3] they aim at it,
And botch the words up[4] fit to their own thoughts;
Which, as her winks and nods and gestures yield them,
Indeed would make one think there might be thought,[5]
Though nothing sure, yet much unhappily.
'Twere good she were spoken with; for she may strew
Dangerous conjectures in ill-breeding minds.

       QUEEN.

Let her come in.   [*Exit* HORATIO.

To my sick soul, as sin's true nature is,
Each toy[6] seems prologue to some great amiss:[7]
So full of artless jealousy[8] is guilt,
It spills itself in fearing to be spilt.

      Enter HORATIO, *with* OPHELIA *distracted.*

       OPHELIA.

Where is the beauteous majesty of Denmark?

       QUEEN.

How now, Ophelia!

       OPHELIA [*sings*].

         How should I your true-love know
            From another one?
         By his cockle hat[9] and staff,
            And his sandal shoon.[10]

---

[1] tricks i'th'world: wickedness and deception in the world. [2] Spurns enviously at straws: shies suspiciously at the most innocent things. [3] collection: to try to collect some meaning from it. [4] botch the words up: twist the meaning of the words. [5] thought: sense. [6] toy: trifle. [7] amiss: misfortune; disaster. [8] jealousy: suspicion. [9] cockle hat: a pilgrim wore a cockle shell in his hat to signify that he had been, or was going, beyond the seas (Holy Land). [10] shoon: shoes.

QUEEN.

las, sweet lady, what imports this song? [1]

OPHELIA.

ay you? nay, pray you, mark.   [*Sings.*

> He is dead and gone, lady,
>   He is dead and gone;
> At his head a grass-green turf,
>   At his heels a stone.

QUEEN.

Jay, but, Ophelia,—

OPHELIA.

ray you, mark.   [*Sings.*

> White his shroud as the mountain snow,

Enter KING.

QUEEN.

las, look here, my lord.

OPHELIA [*sings*].

> Larded [2] with sweet flowers;
> Which bewept to the grave did go
> With true-love showers.

KING.

Iow do you, pretty lady?

OPHELIA.

Vell, God 'ild you! [3] They say the owl was a baker's daugh-
er.[4] Lord, we know what we are, but know not what we may
e. God be at your table!

KING.

Conceit upon her father.[5]

OPHELIA.

ray you, let's have no words of this; but when they ask you
hat it means, say you this:

> To-morrow is Saint Valentine's day,

---

what imports this song: what does this song mean. [2] larded:
arnished; decorated. [3] God 'ild you: God yield you or reward
ou. [4] the owl was a baker's daugh-/ter: an allusion to a folk tale in
hich Jesus asked for bread and when the baker's wife started
give it to Him, the baker's daughter objected, for which she
as changed into an owl. [5] Conceit upon her father: the King
tributes Ophelia's aimless remarks as being caused by grief
ver her father's death.

> All in the morning betime,[1]
> And I a maid at your window,
>> To be your Valentine.[2]
> Then up he rose, and donn'd his clothes,
>> And dupt the chamber-door;
> Let in the maid, that out a maid
>> Never departed more.

KING.

Pretty Ophelia!

OPHELIA.

Indeed, la, without an oath, I'll make an end on't: [*Sing*

> By Gis and by Saint Charity,
>> Alack, and fie for shame!
> Young men will do't, if they come to't;
>> By cock, they are to blame.
> Quoth she, before you tumbled me,
>> You promised me to wed.

He answers:

> So would I ha' done, by yonder sun,
>> An thou hadst not come to my bed.

KING.

How long hath she been thus?

OPHELIA.

I hope all will be well. We must be patient: but I canno
choose but weep, to think they should lay him i'th'col
ground. My brother shall know of it: and so I thank you fo
your good counsel.—Come, my coach!—Good night, ladie
good night, sweet ladies; good night, good night.   [*Exit*

KING.

Follow her close;[3] give her good watch, I pray you.

                                        [*Exit* HORATIO

---

[1] betime: early.
[2] And I a maid at your window,/To be your Valentine: this re
fers to an old custom that the first girl seen by a man on S
Valentine's Day would be his true love.
[3] close: secretly.

this is the poison of deep grief; it springs
from her father's death. O Gertrude, Gertrude,
hen sorrows come, they come not single spies,
t in battalions! [1] First, her father slain:
xt, your son gone; and he most violent author
his own just remove:[2] the people muddied,[3]
ick and unwholesome in their thoughts and whispers,
r good Polonius' death; and we have done but greenly,[4]
hugger-mugger[5] to inter him: poor Ophelia
vided from herself and her fair judgement,
ithout the which we are pictures, or mere beasts:
st, and as much containing as all these,
r brother is in secret come from France;
eds on his wonder,[6] keep himself in clouds,[7]
d wants not buzzers[8] to infect his ear
ith pestilent speeches of his father's death;
herein necessity, of matter beggar'd,[9]
ll nothing stick our person to arraign
ear and ear. O my dear Gertrude, this,
to a murdering-piece,[10] in many places
ves me superfluous death.   [A *noise within.*

QUEEN.

Alack, what noise is this?

KING.

ere are my Switzers?[11] Let them guard the door.

Enter a GENTLEMAN.

aat is the matter?

GENTLEMAN.

Save yourself, my lord:
e ocean, overpeering of his list,[12]
ts not the flats[13] with more impetuous haste

---

t single spies,/But in battalions: a reference to spies coming
advance of an army. [2] just remove: warranted removal. [3] mud-
d: confused. [4] done but greenly: only acted unwisely. [5] hugger-
gger: secretly and hurriedly. [6] wonder: doubts and amazement.
eps himself in the clouds: hold himself aloof. [8] buzzers: tale-
rers. [9] beggard'd: with nothing to support it. [10] murdering-piece:
annon loaded with small ammunition, or canister shot. [11] Switzers:
iss guards. [12] overpeering of his list: rising above its boundary.
ats not the flats: does not submerge the beach.

Than young Laertes, in a riotous head,[1]
O'erbears your officers. The rabble call him lord;
And, as the world were now but to begin,
Antiquity forgot, custom not known,
The ratifiers and props of every word,
They cry, 'Choose we; Laertes shall be king!'
Caps, hands, and tongues applaud it to the clouds,
'Laertes shall be king, Laertes king!'

QUEEN.

How cheerfully on the false trail they cry!
O, this is counter,[2] you false Danish dogs!

KING.

The doors are broke.   [*Noise withi*

Enter LAERTES, *arm'd;* DANES *following.*

LAERTES.

Where is this king?—Sirs, stand you all without.

DANES.

No, let's come in.

LAERTES.

I pray you, give me leave.

DANES.

We will, we will.   [*They retire without the doo*

LAERTES.

I thank you:—keep the door.—O thou vile king,
Give me my father!

QUEEN.

Calmly, good Laertes.

LAERTES.

That drop of blood that's calm proclaims me bastard;
Cries cuckold to my father; brands the harlot
Even here, between the chaste unsmirched [3] brow
Of my true mother.

---

[1] **riotous head:** armed band of ruffians.
[2] **counter:** a hunting term which means tracking or pursuing in t
wrong direction.
[3] **unsmirched:** unsullied; unstained.

KING.

What is the cause, Laertes,
That thy rebellion looks so giant-like?—
Let him go, Gertrude; do not fear our person:
There's such divinity doth hedge[1] a king,
That treason can but peep[2] to what it would,
Acts little of his will.—Tell me, Laertes,
Why thou art thus incensed:—let him go, Gertrude:—
Speak, man.

LAERTES.

Where is my father?

KING.

Dead.

QUEEN.

But not by him.

KING.

Let him demand his fill.

LAERTES.

How came he dead? I'll not be juggled with:
To hell, allegiance! vows, to the blackest devil!
Conscience and grace, to the profoundest pit!
I dare damnation:—to this point I stand,—
That both the worlds[3] I give to negligence,
Let come what comes; only I'll be revenged
Most throughly[4] for my father.

KING.

Who shall stay you?[5]

LAERTES.

My will, not all the world:[6]
And for my means, I'll husband them so well,
They shall go far with little.

KING.

Good Laertes,

---

hedge: surround; protect. [2] can but peep: can only sight him as
from a distance and do no harm. [3] both the worlds: this world and
the next. [4] throughly: thoroughly. [5] stay you: hinder you. [6] My
will, not all the world: it is my will, and nothing in the world
shall stop me.

If you desire to know the certainty
Of your dear father's death, is't writ in your revenge,
That, swoopstake,[1] you will draw both friend and foe,
Winner and loser?

LAERTES.

None but his enemies.

KING.

                Will you know them, then?

LAERTES.

To his good friends thus wide I'll ope[2] my arms,
And, like the kind life-rendering pelican,[3]
Repast them with my blood.

KING.

               Why, now you speak
Like a good child and a true gentleman.
That I am guiltless of your father's death,
And am most sensibly in grief for it,
It shall as level to your judgement 'pear
As day does to your eye.

DANES [*within*].

               Let her come in.

LAERTES.

How now! what noise is that?

Enter OPHELIA.

O heat, dry up my brains! tears seven-times salt,
Burn out the sense and virtue[4] of mine eye!—
By heaven, thy madness shall be paid by weight,
Till our scale turn the beam. O rose of May!
Dear maid, kind sister, sweet Ophelia!—
O heavens! is't possible a young maid's wits

---

[1] swoopstake: that is, like a gambler who insists on taking the
stakes whether he has won or not.
[2] ope: open.
[3] life-rendering pelican: it was an old belief that the pelican would
pierce her own breast to feed her young with her blood.
[4] virtue: power.

ould be as mortal as an old man's life?

ature is fine in love; and, where 'tis fine,

sends some precious instance[1] of itself

ter the thing it loves.

   OPHELIA [*sings*].

       They bore him barefaced on the bier;

       Hey non nonny, nonny, hey nonny;

       And in his grave rain'd many a tear,—

re you well, my dove!

   LAERTES.

adst thou thy wits, and didst persuade revenge,

could not move thus.

   OPHELIA.

ou must sing, 'Down a-down, an you call him a-down-a'[2] O,

w the wheel[3] becomes it! It is the false steward, that stole

s master's daughter.

   LAERTES.

his nothing's more than matter.[4]

   OPHELIA.

here's rosemary, that's for remembrance; pray you, love,

member: and there is pansies, that's for thoughts.

   LAERTES.

document[5] in madness,—thoughts and remembrance fitted.

   OPHELIA.

here's fennel for you, and columbines:—there's rue for you;

d here's some for me:—we may call it herb-grace o' Sun-

ys:—O, you must wear your rue with a difference.[6]—

here's a daisy:—I would give you some violets, but they

ither'd all when my father died:—they say he made a good

d,—   [*Sings.*

---

nstance: sample. [2] 'Down-a-down, and you call him a-down-a.':
e words of a song, but Ophelia is thinking of her father. [3] wheel:
inning wheel, at which Ophelia imagines herself to be sitting.
matter: sense; meaning. [5] document: lesson. [6] with a difference:
r a different reason.

         For bonny sweet Robin is all my joy,—

LAERTES.

Thought and affliction, passion, hell itself,
She turns to favour[1] and to prettiness.

     OPHELIA [*sings*].

            And will a'[2] not come again?
            And will a' not come again?
              No, no, he is dead:
              Go to thy death-bed:
            He never will come again.

            His beard was as white as snow,
            All flaxen was his poll:[3]
              He is gone, he is gone,
              And we cast away moan:
            God ha' mercy on his soul!

And of all[4] Christian souls, I pray God.—God be wi'you.

                                           [*Exit.*

LAERTES.

Do you see this, O God?

     KING.

Laertes, I must commune with your grief,
Or you deny me right. Go but apart,
Make choice of whom your wisest friends you will,
And they shall hear and judge 'twixt you and me:
If by direct or by collateral[5] hand
They find us toucht,[6] we will our kingdom give,
Our crown, our life, and all that we call ours,
To you in satisfaction; but if not,
Be you content to lend your patience to us,
And we shall jointly labour with your soul
To give it due content.

---

[1] **favour:** attractiveness.
[2] **a':** he.
[3] **poll:** head
[4] **of all:** for all.
[5] **collateral:** indirect.
[6] **toucht:** implicated; accessory to the crime.

LAERTES.

        Let this be so;

His means of death,[1] his obscure burial,—

No trophy, sword, nor hatchment[2] o'er his bones,

No noble rite nor formal ostentation,[3]—

Cry to be heard, as 'twere from heaven to earth,

That I must call't in question.

KING.

                So you shall;

And where th'offence is let the great axe fall.

I pray you, go with me.   [*Exeunt.*

Scene VI.

Another room in the castle.

Enter HORATIO *and a* SERVANT.

HORATIO.

What are they that would speak with me?

SERVANT.

Seafaring men, sir: they say they have letters for you.

HORATIO.

Let them come in.—   [*Exit* SERVANT.

I do not know from what part of the world

I should be greeted, if not from Lord Hamlet.

Enter SAILORS.

FIRST SAILOR.

God bless you, sir.

HORATIO.

Let Him bless thee too.

FIRST SAILOR.

He shall, sir, an't please Him. There's a letter for you, sir,—
it comes from the ambassador that was bound for England,
—if your name be Horatio, as I am let to know[4] it is.

---

[1] His means of death: the means of his death.

[2] hatchment: armorial escutcheon used at funerals; panel upon
which the arms of the diseased were displayed.

[3] formal ostentation: funeral pomp.

[4] let to know: made to know.

HORATIO [*reads*].

Horatio, when thou shalt have overlookt this, give these fellows some means to the king: they have letters for him. Ere we were two days old at sea, a pirate of very warlike appointment[1] gave us chase. Finding ourselves too slow of sail, we put on a compell'd valour;[2] and in the grapple I boarded them: on the instant they got clear of our ship; so I alone became their prisoner. They have dealt with me like thieves of mercy:[3] but they knew what they did; I am to do a good turn for them. Let the king have the letters I have sent; and repair thou to me with as much speed as thou wouldest fly death. I have words to speak in thine ear will make thee dumb; yet are they much too light for the bore of the matter.[4] These good fellows will bring thee where I am. Rosencrantz and Guildenstern hold their course for England: of them I have much to tell thee. Farewell.

He that thou knowest thine, HAMLET.

Come, I will make you way[5] for these your letters;
And do't the speedier, that you may direct me
To him from whom you brought them. [*Exeunt.*

SCENE VII.

Another room in the castle.

Enter KING *and* LAERTES.

KING.

Now must your conscience my acquittance seal,
And you must put me in your heart for friend,

---

[1] appointment: equipment.
[2] compell'd valour: forced bravery.
[3] thieves of mercy: merciful thieves.
[4] too light for the bore of the matter: literally too light for the caliber of the gun; not grave enough for the facts to be discussed.
[5] make you way: gain you admittance.

Sith[1] you have heard, and with a knowing ear,
That he which hath your noble father slain
Pursued my life.

LAERTES.

It well appears:—but tell me
Why you proceeded not against these feats,
So crimeful [2] and so capital in nature,
As by your safety, wisdom, all things else,
You mainly were stirr'd up.[3]

KING.

O, for two special reasons;
Which may to you, perhaps, seem much unsinew'd,[4]
But yet to me th' [5] are strong. The queen his mother
Lives almost by his looks; and for myself,—
My virtue or my plague, be it either which,—
She's so conjunctive[6] to my life and soul,
That, as the star moves not but in his sphere,
I could not but by her. The other motive,
Why to a public count[7] I might not go,
Is the great love the general gender[8] bear him;
Who, dipping all his faults in their affection,
Would, like the spring that turneth wood to stone,
Convert his gyves[9] to graces; so that my arrows,
Too slightly timber'd for so loud a wind,
Would have reverted to my bow again,
And not where I had aim'd them.

LAERTES.

And so have I a noble father lost;
A sister driven into desperate terms,—
Whose worth, if praises may go back again,
Stood challenger on mount of all the age
For her perfections:—but my revenge will come.

Sith: since. [2] crimeful: criminal. [3] You mainly were stirr'd up:
you were chiefly involved. [4] unsinew'd: weak. [5] th': they. [6] conjunctive: closely united; joined. [7] count: account; trial. [8] general
gender: the masses. [9] gyves: fetters.

KING.
Break not your sleeps for that: you must not think
That we are made of stuff so flat and dull,
That we can let our beard be shook with danger,
And think it pastime. You shortly shall hear more:
I loved your father, and we love ourself;
And that, I hope, will teach you to imagine—

Enter a MESSENGER

How now! what news?

MESSENGER.
                Letters my lord, from Hamlet:
This to your majesty; this to the queen.

KING.
From Hamlet! who brought them?

MESSENGER.
Sailors, my lord, they say; I saw them not:
They were given me by Claudio,—he received them
Of him that brought them.

KING.
              Laertes, you shall hear them.—
Leave us.   [*Exit* MESSENGER
[*Reads*] High and mighty,—You shall know I am set naked [1]
on your kingdom. To-morrow shall I beg leave to see your
kingly eyes: when I shall, first asking your pardon there-
unto, recount the occasion of my sudden and more strange
return.

                               HAMLET.

What should this mean? Are all the rest come back?
Or is it some abuse,[2] and no such thing?

LAERTES.
Know you the hand?

---

[1] naked: defenseless; alone.
[2] abuse: deception.

KING.

                  'Tis Hamlet's character:[1]—'Naked,'—
And in a postscript here, he says, 'alone.'
Can you advise me?

LAERTES.

I'm lost in it, my lord. But let him come;
It warms the very sickness in my heart,
That I shall live and tell him to his teeth,
'Thus diddest thou.'

KING.

               If it be so, Laertes,—
As how should it be so? how otherwise?—
Will you be ruled by me?

LAERTES.

               Ay, my lord;
So[2] you will not o'errule me to a peace.

KING.

To thine own peace. If he be now return'd,—
As checking at[3] his voyage, and that he means
No more to undertake it,—I will work him
To an exploit, now ripe in my device,[4]
Under the which he shall not choose but fall:
And for his death no wind of blame shall breathe;
But even his mother shall uncharge the practice,[5]
And call it accident.

LAERTES.

              My lord, I will be ruled;
The rather, if you could devise it so,
That I might be the organ.

KING.

               It falls right.[6]
You have been talkt of since your travel much,
And that in Hamlet's hearing, for a quality

---

[1] character: handwriting.
[2] So: provided that.
[3] checking at: turning away from (a term in falconry).
[4] device: plan; scheme.
[5] uncharge the practice: not accuse anyone of the plot.
[6] falls right: fits in.

Wherein, they say, you shine: your sum of parts[1]
Did not together pluck such envy from him,
As did that one; and that, in my regard,
Of the unworthiest siege.[2]

LAERTES.

What part is that, my lord?

KING.

A very riband [3] in the cap of youth,
Yet needful too; for youth no less becomes
The light and careless livery[4] that it wears
Than settled age his sables and his weeds,[5]
Importing health and graveness.—Two months since,
Here was a gentleman of Normandy,—
I've seen myself, and served against, the French,
And they can well on horseback: but this gallant
Had witchcraft in't; he grew unto his seat;
And to such wondrous doing brought his horse,
As he had been incorpsed and demi-natured [6]
With the brave[7] beast: so far he topt[8] my thought,
That I, in forgery[9] of shapes and tricks,
Come short of what he did.

LAERTES.

A Norman was't?

KING.

A Norman.

LAERTES.

Upon my life, Lamond.

KING.

The very same.

LAERTES.

I know him well: he is the brooch, indeed,
And gem of all the nation.

---

[1] your sum of parts: all your qualities. [2] unworthiest siege: lowest rank. [3] riband: ribbon. [4] livery: dress. [5] weeds: decorous garments. [6] As he had been incorpsed and demi-natured: as if man and horse were one body, half man, half horse. [7] brave: noble; handsome. [8] topt: surpassed; went beyond. [9] forgery: imitation.

KING.

He made confession of you;[1]
And gave you such a masterly report,[2]
For art and exercise in your defence,
And for your rapier most especially,
That he cried out, 'twould be a sight indeed,
If one could match you: the scrimers[3] of their nation,
He swore, had neither motion, guard, nor eye,
If you opposed them. Sir, this report of his
Did Hamlet so envenom with his envy,
That he could nothing do but wish and beg
Your sudden coming o'er, to play with him.
Now, out of this,—

LAERTES.

                What out of this, my lord?

KING.

Laertes, was your father dear to you?
Or are you like the painting of a sorrow,
A face without a heart?

LAERTES.

                Why ask you this?

KING.

Not that I think you did not love your father;
But that I know love is begun by time;
And that I see, in passages of proof,[4]
Time qualifies the spark and fire of it.
There lives within the very flame of love
A kind of wick or snuff that will abate it;
And nothing is at a like[5] goodness still;
For goodness, growing to a plurisy,[6]
Dies in his own too-much: that we would do,
We should do when we would; for this 'would' changes,

---

[1] **made confession of you**: admitted your excellence.
[2] **a masterly report**: a report of your mastery.
[3] **scrimers**: fencers.
[4] **passages of proof**: instances to prove it.
[5] **a like**: the same.
[6] **plurisy**: fullness; plethora.

And hath abatements and delays as many
As there are tongues, are hands, are accidents;
And then this 'should' is like a spendthrift sigh,[1]
That hurts by easing. But, to th'quick o'th' ulcer:—
Hamlet comes back: what would you undertake,
To show yourself your father's son in deed
More than in words?

    LAERTES.

               To cut his throat i'th'church.

    KING.

No place, indeed, should murder sanctuarize;
Revenge should have no bounds. But, good Laertes,
Will you do this, keep close within your chamber.
Hamlet return'd shall know you are come home:
We'll put on[2] those shall praise your excellence,
And set a double varnish on the fame
The Frenchman gave you; bring you, in fine,[3] together,
And wager on your heads: he, being remiss,[4]
Most generous, and free from all contriving,
Will not peruse the foils; so that, with ease,
Or with a little shuffling, you may choose
A sword unbated,[5] and, in a pass of practice,[6]
Requite him for your father.

    LAERTES.

               I will do't:
And for that purpose I'll anoint my sword.
I bought an unction[7] of a mountebank,[8]
So mortal,[9] that but dip a knife in it.
Where it draws blood no cataplasm[10] so rare,
Collected from all simples[11] that have virtue[12]

---

[1] a spendthrift sigh: a wasting sigh; it was a common believe during Shakespeare's day that a sigh caused the loss of a drop of blood from the heart. [2] put on: incite. [3] in fine: finally; in the end. [4] remiss: careless. [5] unbated: not blunted by a button fixed to the end of a foil. [6] pass of practice: treacherous thrust while supposedly practicing. [7] unction: ointment. [8] mountebank: quack doctor. [9] mortal: deadly. [10] cataplasm: poultice. [11] simples: herbs. [12] virtue: power.

Under the moon, can save the thing from death
That is but scratcht withal: I'll touch my point
With this contagion, that, if I gall [1] him slightly,
It may be death.

> KING.
>
>   Let's further think of this;
> Weigh what convenience both of time and means
> May fit us to our shape;[2] if this should fail,
> And that our drift look[3] through our bad performance,
> 'Twere better not assay'd: therefore this project
> Should have a back or second, that might hold,
> If this should blast in proof.[4] Soft!—let me see:—
> We'll make a solemn wager on your cunnings,—
> I ha't:[5]
> When in your motion you are hot and dry,—
> As make your bouts more violent to that end,—
> And that he calls for drink, I'll have prepared him
> A chalice for the nonce;[6] whereon but sipping,
> If he by chance escape your venom'd stuck,[7]
> Our purpose may hold [8] there. But stay! what noise?—

> *Enter* QUEEN.

How now, sweet queen!

> QUEEN.
>
> One woe doth tread upon another's heel,
> So fast they follow:—your sister's drown'd, Laertes.

> LAERTES.

Drown'd! O, where?

> QUEEN.
>
> There is a willow grows aslant[9] a brook,
> That shows his hoar[10] leaves in a glassy stream;

---

[1] **gall**: prick. [2] **fit us to our shape**: suit our plan. [3] **drift look**: our purpose show itself. [4] **blast in proof**: literally, exlode in the test. [5] **ha't**: have it. [6] **nonce**: for the occasion. [7] **stuck**: thrust. [8] **hold**: succeed. [9] **aslant**: bending over. [10] **hoar**: silvery-gray color on the underside.

There with fantastic garlands did she come
Of crow-flowers,[1] nettles, daisies, and long purples[2]
That liberal[3] shepherds give a grosser name,
But our cold maids do dead men's fingers call them:
There, on the pendent boughs her coronet weeds[4]
Clambering to hang, an envious sliver[5] broke;
When down her weedy trophies and herself
Fell in the weeping brook. Her clothes spread wide,
And, mermaid-like, awhile they bore her up;
Which time she chanted snatches of old tunes,
As one incapable of her own distress,
Or like a creature native and indued [6]
Unto that element: but long it could not be
Till that her garments, heavy with their drink,
Pull'd the poor wretch from her melodious lay[7]
To muddy death.

LAERTES.
                    Alas, then, she is drown'd?

QUEEN.
Drown'd, drown'd.

LAERTES.
Too much of water hast thou, poor Ophelia,
And therefore I forbid my tears: but yet
It is our trick,[8] nature her custom holds,
Let shame say what it will: when these are gone,
The woman will be out.[9]—Adieu, my lord:
I have a speech of fire, that fain would blaze,
But that this folly douts[10] it.   [Exit.

KING.
                    Let's follow, Gertrude:
How much I had to do to calm his rage!
Now fear I this will give it start again;
Therefore let's follow.   [Exeunt.

---

[1] crow-flowers: crowfoot; probably wild hyacinth. [2] long purples:
purple orchids. [3] liberal: free-spoken. [4] coronet weeds: flowers
woven into a crown. [5] sliver: small branch. [6] indued: suited; at
home. [7] lay: song. [8] trick: habit. [9] the woman will be out: his wo-
manly tears will be exhausted. [10] douts: extinguishes.

Hamlet

ACT 5

ACT V

HORATIO AND Hamlet, on their way to Elsinore, pass throu[gh]
the graveyard where Ophelia will be buried. Hamlet, engag[ed]
in grim banter with one of the gravediggers, is suddenly i[n]
terrupted by Ophelia's funeral procession. Laertes' loud pr[o]
testations of grief inflame Hamlet, and he leaps into Opheli[a's]
grave to grapple with her brother. They are separated a[nd]
all return to the castle where Hamlet tells Horatio how [he]
has changed Claudius' letter, instructing the King of Engla[nd]
to kill Rosencrantz and Guildenstern. Hamlet receives an i[n]
vitation to duel with Laertes before the court, and agrees [in]
spite of the protestations of Horatio. The match appears [to]
be going well for Hamlet when his mother, drinking to h[is]
health, unsuspectingly uses the poisoned cup. Laertes, de[s]
perate, pricks Hamlet with the poisoned sword, and in th[e]
ensuing scuffle loses the weapon to Hamlet, who wounds hi[m]
with it. The queen dies, and Laertes, repenting of h[is]
treachery, tells Hamlet of the plot. In a frenzy, Hamlet ru[ns]
Claudius through with his sword, then forces the poison[ed]
drink down his throat. As the flourishes of Fortinbras' a[p]
proaching army are heard, Hamlet dies, leaving Horatio [to]
tell his story and voice his approval of Fortinbras as success[or]
to the Danish throne.

ACT V. Scene I.

Elsinore. A churchyard.

Enter two CLOWNS, with spades, &c.

FIRST CLOWN.

Is she to be buried in Christian burial that wilfully seeks her own salvation?

SECOND CLOWN.

I tell thee she is; and therefore make her grave straight:[1] the crowner[2] hath sat on her,[3] and finds it Christian burial.

FIRST CLOWN.

How can that be, unless she drown'd herself in her own defence?

SECOND CLOWN.

Why, 'tis found so.

---

[1] **straight:** immediately; Johnson interprets this word as meaning in a direct line, parallel with the church.

[2] **crowner:** coroner.

[3] **sat on her:** judged her case.

FIRST CLOWN.

It must be *se offendendo;*[1] it cannot be else. For here lies the point: if I drown myself wittingly, it argues an act: and an act hath three branches; it is, to act, to do, to perform: argal,[2] she drown'd herself wittingly.

SECOND CLOWN.

Nay, but hear you, goodman delver,—

FIRST CLOWN.

Give me leave.[3] Here lies the water; good: here stands the man; good: if the man go to this water and drown himself, it is, will he, nill he,[4] he goes,—mark you that; but if the water come to him and drown him, he drowns not himself: argal, he that is not guilty of his own death shortens not his own life.

SECOND CLOWN.

But is this law?

FIRST CLOWN.

Ay, marry, is't; crowner's quest-law.[5]

SECOND CLOWN.

Will you ha' the truth on't? If this had not been a gentlewoman, she should have been buried out o' Christian burial.

---

[1] *se offendendo:* the clown's garbled version of *se defendendo*— in self-defense.

[2] argal: therefore (another corruption).

[3] give me leave: allow me to continue.

[4] nill he: will he not.

[5] crowner's quest-law: corner's inquest law.

FIRST CLOWN.

hy, there thou sayst: and the more pity that great folk
ould have countenance[1] in this world to drown or hang
emselves, more than their even Christian.[2]—Come, my
ade. There is no ancient gentlemen but gardeners, ditchers,
d grave-makers: they hold up[3] Adam's profession.

SECOND CLOWN.

as he a gentleman?

FIRST CLOWN.

was the first that ever bore arms.[4]

SECOND CLOWN.

hy, he had none.

FIRST CLOWN.

hat, art a heathen? How dost thou understand the Scrip-
re? The Scripture says, Adam digg'd: could he dig without
ms? I'll put another question to thee: if thou answerest me
t to the purpose, confess thyself—

SECOND CLOWN.

o to.[5]

FIRST CLOWN.

hat is he that builds stronger than either the mason, the
ipwright, or the carpenter?

---

ountenance: sanction; encouragement.
ven Christian: fellow Christian.
old up: follow up; continue (Schmidt).
rms: coat of arms; Adam's spade is mentioned in some books of
raldry as the oldest form of escutcheon.
;o to: come now (a common reproof).

SECOND CLOWN.

The gallows-maker; for that frame outlives a thousand tenants.

FIRST CLOWN.

I like thy wit well, in good faith: the gallows does well; but how does it well? it does well to those that do ill: now, thou dost ill to say the gallows is built stronger than the church: argal, the gallows may do well to thee. To't again, come.

SECOND CLOWN.

'Who builds stronger than a mason, a shipwright, or a carpenter?'

FIRST CLOWN.

Ay, tell me that, and unyoke.[1]

SECOND CLOWN.

Marry, now I can tell.

FIRST CLOWN.

To't.

SECOND CLOWN.

Mass,[2] I cannot tell.

Enter HAMLET *and* HORATIO, *afar off.*

FIRST CLOWN.

Cudgel thy brains no more about it, for your dull ass will not mend his pace with beating; and when you are askt this question next, say 'a gravemaker:' the houses that he makes lasts till doomsday. Go, get thee to Yaughan;[3] fetch me a stoop[4] of liquor.   [*Exit* SECOND CLOWN.
            [*He digs, and sings.*

    In youth,[5] when I did love, did love,
        Methought it was very sweet,
    To contract, O, the time, for, ah, my behove,

---

[1] unyoke: literally, unharness; quit. [2] Mass: by the Holy Mass [3] Yaughan: apparently the name of a tavern-keeper. [4] stoop tankard; flagon. [5] In youth, etc.: the disjointed lines of a song by Lord Vaux, "The Aged Lover renounceth Love," from *Tottel* *Miscellany;* the "O" and "ah" have been interpreted by some as grunts of the gravedigger at work.

O, methought there was nothing meet.

HAMLET.

Has this fellow no feeling of his business, that he sings at grave-making?

HORATIO.

Custom hath made it in him a property of easiness.[1]

HAMLET.

'Tis e'en so: the hand of little employment hath the daintier sense.[2]

FIRST CLOWN [sings].

>   But age, with his stealing steps,
>   Hath claw'd me in his clutch,
>   And hath shipt me intil the land,[3]
>   As if I had never been such.

[Throws up a skull.

HAMLET.

That skull had a tongue in it, and could sing once: how the knave jowls[4] it to the ground, as if it were Cain's jaw-bone, that did the first murder! It might be the pate of a politician,[5] which this ass now o'er-reaches;[6] one that would circumvent God, might it not?

HORATIO.

It might, my lord.

HAMLET.

Or of a courtier; which could say 'Good morrow, sweet lord! How dost thou, good lord?' This might be my lord such-a-one, that praised my lord such-a-one's horse, when he meant to beg it,[7]—might it not?

HORATIO.

Ay, my lord.

---

[1] Custom hath made it in him a property of easiness: habit has made it an easy thing for him to do. [2] daintier sense: nicer, more sensitive feeling. [3] hath shipt me intil the land: has buried me in the earth. [4] jowls: knocks; dashes. [5] politician: plotter; schemer. [6] o'er-reaches: takes liberties with; has the better of. [7] beg it: borrow it.

HAMLET.

Why, e'en so: and now my Lady Worm's;[1] chapless,[2] and knockt about the mazard[3] with a sexton's spade: here's fine revolution, an we had the trick[4] to see't. Did these bones cost no more the breeding, but to play at loggats[5] with 'em? mine ache to think on't.

FIRST CLOWN [sings].

> A pickaxe, and a spade, a spade,
>> For and a shrouding-sheet:
> O, a pit of clay for to be made
>> For such a guest is meet.

[Throws up another skull.

HAMLET.

There's another: why may not that be the skull of a lawyer? Where be his quiddits[6] now, his quillets,[7] his cases, his tenures, and his tricks? why does he suffer this rude knave now to knock him about the sconce with a dirty shovel, and will not tell him of his action of battery? Hum! This fellow might be in's time a great buyer of land, with his statutes, his recognizances, his fines, his double vouchers, his recovies: is this the fine of his fines, and the recovery of his recoveries, to have his fine pate full of fine dirt? will his vouchers vouch him no more of his purchases, and double ones too, than the length and breadth of a pair of indentures?[8] The very conveyances[9] of his lands will hardly lie in this box; and must the inheritor himself have no more, ha?

HORATIO.

Not a jot more, my lord.

---

[1] my Lady Worm's: that is, belonging to the worms. [2] chapless: without lower jaws. [3] mazard: head. [4] trick: knack. [5] loggats: an old English game, played with pieces of woods, or small logs, thrown at a mark. [6] quiddits: quiddities: the subtleties of law and logic. [7] quillets: tricks of the trade. [8] indentures: copies of contracts. [9] conveyances: title deeds.

HAMLET.

s not parchment made of sheep-skins?

HORATIO.

Ay, my lord, and of calf-skins too.

HAMLET.

They are sheep and calves which seek out assurance in that. I will speak to this fellow.—Whose grave's this, sirrah?

FIRST CLOWN.

Mine, sir.—   [*Sings.*

O, a pit of clay for to be made
For such a guest is meet.

HAMLET.

I think it be thine, indeed; for thou liest in't.

FIRST CLOWN.

You lie out on't, sir, and therefore it is not yours: for my part, I do not lie in't, and yet it is mine.

HAMLET.

Thou dost lie in't, to be in't, and say it is thine: 'tis for the dead, not for the quick;[1] therefore thou liest.

FIRST CLOWN.

'Tis a quick lie, sir; 'twill away again, from me to you.

HAMLET.

What man dost thou dig it for?

FIRST CLOWN.

For no man, sir.

HAMLET.

What woman, then?

FIRST CLOWN.

For none, neither.

HAMLET.

Who is to be buried in't?

---

quick: living.

FIRST CLOWN.

One that was a woman, sir; but, rest her soul, she's dead.

HAMLET.

How absolute[1] the knave is! we must speak by the card,[2] o
equivocation will undo us. By the Lord, Horatio, this three
years I have taken note of it; the age is grown so pickt,[3] tha
the toe of the peasant comes so near the heel of the courtier
he galls his kibe.[4]—How long hast thou been a gravemaker?

FIRST CLOWN.

Of all the days i'th'year, I came to't that day that our las
king Hamlet o'ercame Fortinbras.

HAMLET.

How long is that since?

FIRST CLOWN.

Cannot you tell that? every fool can tell that: it was that ver
day that young Hamlet was born,—he that is mad, and sen
into England.

HAMLET.

Ay, marry, why was he sent into England?

FIRST CLOWN.

Why, because a' was mad: a' shall recover his wits there; or
if a' do not, 'tis no great matter there.

HAMLET.

Why?

FIRST CLOWN.

'Twill not be seen in him there; there the men are as mad a
he.

HAMLET.

How come he mad?

---

[1] absolute: exact; positive.
[2] by the card: to the point; with the greatest precision.
[3] pickt: refined; choosy.
[4] he galls his kibe: he chafes or rubs against his chilblain.

FIRST CLOWN.

Very strangely, they say.

HAMLET.

How strangely?

FIRST CLOWN.

Faith, e'en with losing his wits.

HAMLET.

Upon what ground?

FIRST CLOWN.

Why, here in Denmark: I have been sexton here, man and
boy, thirty years.

HAMLET.

How long will a man lie i'th'earth ere he rot?

FIRST CLOWN.

I'faith, if a' be not rotten before a' die,—as we have many
pocky corses[1] now-a-days that will scarce hold the laying in,—
a' will last you some eight year or nine year: a tanner will last
you nine year.

HAMLET.

Why he more than another?

FIRST CLOWN.

Why, sir, his hide is so tann'd with his trade that a' will keep
out water a great while; and your water is a sore[2] decayer of
your whoreson[3] dead body. Here's a skull now hath lain you
i'th'earth three-and-twenty years.

HAMLET.

Whose was it?

FIRST CLOWN.

A whoreson mad fellow's it was: whose do you think it was?

HAMLET.

Nay, I know not.

---

[1] pocky corses: i.e., the corpses of those that have died of a wasting disease.

[2] sore: grievous.

[3] whoreson: literally, bastard (a popular term of derision).

FIRST CLOWN.

A pestilence on him for a mad rogue! a' pour'd a flagon of Rhenish[1] on my head once. This same skull, sir, was Yorick's skull, the king's jester.

HAMLET.

This?

FIRST CLOWN.

E'en that.

HAMLET.

Let me see. [*Takes the skull.*]—Alas, poor Yorick!—I knew him, Horatio: a fellow of infinite jest, of most excellent fancy: he hath borne me on his back a thousand times; and now, how abhorred in my imagination it is! my gorge rises at it. Here hung those lips that I have kist I know not how oft. Where be your gibes now? your gambols? your songs? your flashes of merriment, that were wont to set the table on a roar? Not one now, to mock your own grinning? quite chop-faln?[2] Now get you to my lady's chamber, and tell her, let her paint an inch thick, to this favour[3] she must come; make her laugh at that.—Prithee, Horatio, tell me one thing.

HORATIO.

What's that, my lord?

HAMLET.

Dost thou think Alexander lookt o' this fashion i'th'earth?

HORATIO.

E'en so.

HAMLET.

And smelt so? pah!   [*Puts down the skull.*

---

[1] Rhenish: wine.
[2] chop-faln: jawless.
[3] favour; personal appearance.

HORATIO.

E'en so, my lord.

HAMLET.

To what base uses we may return, Horatio! Why may not imagination trace the noble dust of Alexander till he find it stopping a bung-hole?

HORATIO.

Twere to consider too curiously, to consider so.[1]

HAMLET.

No, faith, not a jot; but to follow him thither with modesty enough,[2] and likelihood to lead it: as thus; Alexander died, Alexander was buried, Alexander returneth into dust; the dust is earth: of earth we make loam; and why of that loam whereto he was converted might they not stop a beer-barrel?

> Imperious[3] Caesar, dead and turn'd to clay,
> Might stop a hole to keep the wind away:
> O, that that earth which kept the world in awe
> Should patch a wall t'expel the winter's flaw![4]—

But soft! but soft! aside:—here comes the king,

Enter KING, QUEEN, LAERTES *and the Corse;* PRIESTS *and* LORDS *attendant.*

The queen, the courtiers: who is that they follow?
And with such maimed[5] rites? This doth betoken
The corse they follow did with desperate hand
Fordo[6] its own life: 'twas of some estate.
Couch[7] we awhile, and mark.   [*Retiring with* HORATIO.

LAERTES.

What ceremony else?

HAMLET.

That is Laertes,
A very noble youth: mark.

---

[1] Twere to consider too curiously, to consider so: it would be too fanciful to think in this way. [2] modesty enough: without exaggeration. [3] Imperious: imperial. [4] flaw: gust of wind. [5] maimed: imperfect; poor. [6] Fordo: to take; destroy. [7] Couch: hide.

LAERTES.

What ceremony else?

FIRST PRIEST.

Her obsequies have been as far enlarged
As we have warrantise:[1] her death was doubtful;
And, but that great command o'ersways the order,
She should in ground unsanctified have lodged
Till the last trumpet; for charitable prayers,
Shards,[2] flints, and pebbles should be thrown on her:
Yet here she is allow'd her virgin crants,[3]
Her maiden strewments,[4] and the bringing home
Of bell [5] and burial.

LAERTES.

Must there no more be done?

FIRST PRIEST.

                       No more be done:
We should profane the service of the dead
To sing a requiem, and such rest to her
As to peace-parted souls.

LAERTES.

                  Lay her i'th'earth;—
And from her fair and unpolluted flesh
May violets spring!—I tell thee, churlish priest,
A ministering angel shall my sister be,
When thou liest howling.[6]

HAMLET.

                What, the fair Ophelia!

QUEEN.

Sweets to the sweet: farewell!   [*Scattering flowers*
I hoped thou shouldst have been my Hamlet's wife;
I thought thy bride-bed to have deckt, sweet maid,

---

[1] **warrantise**: warranty.
[2] **shards**: broken bits of pottery.
[3] **virgin crants**: the garlands and wreaths of a maiden.
[4] **strewments**: flowers strewn on her grave.
[5] **bell**: the tolling of the funeral bell.
[6] **howling**: wailing in hell.

And not have strew'd thy grave.

LAERTES.
                  O, treble woe
Fall ten times treble on that cursed head
Whose wicked deed thy most ingenious sense[1]
Depriv'd thee of!—Hold off the earth awhile,
Till I have caught her once more in mine arms:
                        [*Leaps into the grave.*
Now pile your dust upon the quick and dead,
Till of this flat a mountain you have made
To'ertop old Pelion[2] or the skyish head
Of blue Olympus.

HAMLET [*advancing*].
            What is he whose grief
Bears such an emphasis; whose phrase of sorrow
Conjures the wandering stars,[3] and makes them stand
Like wonder-wounded [4] hearers? This is I,
Hamlet the Dane.   [*Leaps into the grave.*

LAERTES.
          The devil take thy soul!
                    [*Grappling with him*

HAMLET.
Thou pray'st not well.
I prithee, take thy fingers from my throat;
For, though I am not splenitive[5] and rash,
Yet have I something in me dangerous,
Which let thy wisdom fear: hold off thy hand!

KING.
Pluck them asunder.

QUEEN.
         Hamlet, Hamlet!

---

[1] ingenious sense: clever mind. [2] Pelion: the Titons, warring with
the gods, whose home was on Olympus, piled two mountain peaks,
Pelion and Ossa, on top of each other in trying to reach Olympus.
[3] wandering stars: the planets. [4] wonder-wounded: awe-striken.
[5] splenitive: quick-tempered.

ALL.

               Gentlemen,—

HORATIO.

Good my lord, be quiet.

 [*The* ATTENDANTS *part them, and they come out of the grave.*

HAMLET.

Why, I will fight with him upon this theme
Until my eyelids will no longer wag.

QUEEN.

O my son, what theme?

HAMLET.

I loved Ophelia: forty thousand brothers
Could not, with all their quantity of love,
Make up my sum.—What wilt thou do for her?

KING.

O, he is mad, Laertes.

QUEEN.

For love of God, forbear him.[1]

HAMLET.

'Swounds,[2] show me what thou'lt do:
Woo't[3] weep? woo't fight? woo't fast? woo't tear thyself?
Woo't drink up eisel?[4] eat a crocodile?
I'll do't.—Dost thou come here to whine?
To outface me with leaping in her grave?
Be buried quick[5] with her, and so will I:
And if thou prate[6] of mountains, let them throw
Millions of acres on us, till our ground,
Singeing his pate against the burning zone,[7]
Make Ossa like a wart! Nay, an thou'lt mouth,
I'll rant as well as thou.

---

[1] forbear him: humor him. [2] 'swounds: an oath—God's wounds.
[3] Woo't: wouldst thou. [4] drink up eisel: quaff down vinegar.
[5] quick: alive. [6] prate: talk wildly. [7] the burning zone: the sun.

QUEEN.

              This is mere madness:
And thus awhile the fit will work on him;
Anon, as patient as the female dove
When that her golden couplets[1] are disclosed,
His silence will sit drooping.

HAMLET.

                Hear you, sir;
What is the reason that you use me thus?
I loved you ever: but it is no matter;
Let Hercules himself do what he may,
The cat will mew, and dog will have his day.   [*Exit.*

KING.

I pray you, good Horatio, wait upon him.—   [*Exit* HORATIO.
[*to* LAERTES] Strengthen your patience in our last night's
    speech;
We'll put the matter to the present push.[2]—
Good Gertrude, set some watch over your son.—
This grave shall have a living monument:
An hour of quiet shortly shall we see;
Till then, in patience our proceeding be.   [*Exeunt.*

SCENE II.

A hall in the castle.

Enter HAMLET *and* HORATIO.

HAMLET.

So much for this, sir: now shall you see the other;—
You do remember all the circumstance?

HORATIO.

Remember it, my lord!

---

golden couplet: the dove lays only two eggs, which when hatched
are covered with yellow down.
present push: immediate trial.

HAMLET.

Sir, in my heart there was a kind of fighting,
That would not let me sleep: methought I lay
Worse than the mutines[1] in the bilboes.[2] Rashly,
And praised be rashness for it, let us know,
Our indiscretion sometime serves us well,
When our deep plots do pall:[3] and that should learn[4] us
There's a divinity that shapes our ends,
Rough-hew them how we will,—

HORATIO.

That is most certain.

HAMLET.

Up from my cabin,
My sea-grown scarft about me, in the dark
Groped I to find out them: had my desire;
Finger'd their packet; and, in fine, withdrew
To mine own room again: making so bold,
My fears forgetting manners, to unseal
Their grand commission; where I found, Horatio,—
O royal knavery!—an exact command,—
Larded [5] with many several sorts of reasons,
Importing[6] Denmark's health, and England's too,
With, ho! such bugs[7] and goblins in my life,—
That, on the supervise,[8] no leisure bated,[9]
No, not to stay the grinding of the axe,
My head should be struck off.

HORATIO.

Is't possible?

Here's the commission: read it at more leisure.
But wilt thou hear me how I did proceed?

---

[1] mutines: mutineers. [2] bilboes: iron bars with fetters to shackle
disorderly sailors together on shipboard (the name is derived from
Bilboa, Spain). [3] pall: fail. [4] learn: teach. [5] larded: garnished;
greased. [6] importing: regarding. [7] bugs: bugbears. [8] supervise: perusal. [9] no leisure bated: without the slightest delay.

HORATIO.

I beseech you.

HAMLET.

Being thus be-netted round with villainies,—
Ere I could make a prologue to my brains,
They had begun the play,[1]—I sat me down;
Devised a new commission; wrote it fair:—
I once did hold it, as our statists[2] do,
A baseness to write fair, and labour'd much
How to forget that learning; but, sir, now
It did me yeoman's service:[3]—wilt thou know
The effect of what I wrote?

HORATIO.

              Ay, good my lord.·

HAMLET.

An earnest conjuration from the king,—
As England was his faithful tributary;
As love between them like the palm might flourish;
As peace should still her wheaten garland [4] wear,
And stand a comma[5] 'tween their amities,
And many such-like As-es[6] of great charge,[7]—
That, on the view and knowing of these contents,
Without debatement further, more or less,
He should the bearers put to sudden death,
Not shriving-time allow'd.[8]

HORATIO.

              How was this seal'd?

HAMLET.

Why, even in that was heaven ordinant.[9]
I had my father's signet in my purse,
Which was the model of that Danish seal;
Folded the writ[10] up in the form of th'other;

---

[1] **Ere I could make a prologue to my brains,/They had begun the play**: instinctively, without wasting time, my mind began to form a plan. [2] **statists**: statesmen (statesmen left it to their secretaries to write legibly.) [3] **yeoman's service**: freeholders, well-to-do farmers, proved the best troops in the King's service. [4] **wheaten garland**: wheat was both a symbol of peace and of plenty. [5] **comma**: pause. [6] **As-es**: Hamlet has just used "as" in three different instances. [7] **of great charge**: of great weight. [8] **Not shriving-time allow'd**: allowing them no time to confess their sins. [9] **ordinant**: provident. [10] **writ**: commission.

Subscribed it; gave't th'impression; placed it safely,
The changeling[1] never known. Now, the next day
Was our sea-fight; and what to this was sequent[2]
Thou know'st already.

HORATIO.

So Guildenstern and Rosencrantz go to't.[3]

HAMLET.

Why, man, they did make love to this employment;
They are not near my conscience; their defeat
Does by their own insinuation grow:[4]
'Tis dangerous when the baser nature comes
Between the pass[5] and fell [6] incensed points
Of mighty opposites.[7]

HORATIO.

Why, what a king is this!

HAMLET.

Does it not, thinks't thee, stand me now upon,[8]—
He that hath kill'd my king, and whored my mother;
Popt in between th'election and my hopes;
Thrown out his angle for my proper life,
And with such cozenage,[9]—is't not perfect conscience
To quit[10] him with this arm? and is't not to be damn'd
To let this canker of our nature[11] come
In further evil?

HORATIO.

It must be shortly known to him from England
What is the issue of the business there.

---

[1] the changeling: the exchange. [2] what to this was sequent: what ensued. [3] to't: to their death. [4] Does by their own insinuation grow: comes about because of their involvement in this matter. [5] pass: thrust. [6] fell: deadly. [7] opposites: opponents. [8] stand me now upon: becomes my duty now. [9] cozenage: trickery, with a pun on "cousin." [10] quit: requite; finish him off. [11] canker of our nature: sore or cancer of humanity.

HAMLET.

It will be short: the interim is mine;
And a man's life's no more than to say 'one.'
But I am very sorry, good Horatio,
That to Laertes I forgot myself;
For, by the image of my cause, I see
The portraiture of his: I'll court his favours:
But, sure, the bravery[1] of his grief did put me
Into a towering passion.

HORATIO.

Peace! who comes here?
Enter OSRIC.

OSRIC.

Your lordship is right welcome back to Denmark.

HAMLET.

I humbly thank you, sir.—[*aside to* HORATIO]
Dost know this water-fly? [2]

HORATIO [*aside to* HAMLET].

No, my good lord.

HAMLET [*aside to* HORATIO].

Thy state is the more gracious; for 'tis a vice to know him. He
hath much land, and fertile: let a beast be lord of beasts, and
his crib shall stand at the king's mess:[3] 'tis a chough;[4] but, as I
say, spacious in the possession of dirt.[5]

OSRIC.

Sweet lord, if your lordship were at leisure, I should impart
a thing to you from his majesty.

HAMLET.

I will receive it, sir, with all diligence of spirit. Put your
bonnet to his right use; 'tis for the head.

OSRIC.

I thank your lordship, it is very hot.

---

bravery: ostentation; public demonstration. [2] water-fly: busy
trifler; gnat. [3] let a beast be lord of beasts, and/his crib shall stand
at the king's mess: that is, anyone wealthy enough is welcome at
Court. [4] chough: jackdaw (derisive term). [5] spacious in the possession of dirt: i.e., a large landowner.

HAMLET.

No, believe me, 'tis very cold; the wind is northerly.

OSRIC.

It is indifferent cold[1], my lord, indeed.

HAMLET.

But yet methinks it is very sultry and hot for my complexion.[2]

OSRIC.

Exceedingly, my lord; it is very sultry,—as 'twere,—I cannot tell how.—But, my lord, his majesty bade me signify to you, that he has laid a great wager on your head: sir, this is the matter,—

HAMLET.

I beseech you, remember[3]—

[HAMLET *moves him to put on his hat.*

OSRIC.

Nay, good my lord: for mine ease, in good faith. Sir, here is newly come to court Laertes; believe me, an absolute gentleman, full of most excellent differences,[4] of very soft society[5] and great showing;[6] indeed, to speak feelingly of him, he is the card or calendar of gentry,[7] for you shall find in him the continent[8] of what part a gentleman would see.

HAMLET.

Sir, his definement suffers no perdition[9] in you;—though, I know, to divide him inventorially would dizzy the arithmetic of memory, and yet but yaw[10] neither, in respect of his quick sail. But, in the verity of extolment, I take him to be a soul of great article;[11] and his infusion of such dearth and rareness, as, to make true diction of him, his semblable is his

---

[1] **indifferent cold:** somewhat cold. [2] **complexion:** temperament. [3] **I beseech you, remember:** I beg of you, remember your manners. [4] **excellent differences:** distinguishing marks of excellence. [5] **soft society:** courteous or gentle manners. [6] **great showing:** noble bearing. [7] **the card or calendar of gentry:** a perfect model of good breeding. [8] **continent:** possessor. [9] **perdition:** loss. [10] **yaw:** steer wildly (a sailing term). [11] **great article:** great genius.

mirror;[1] and who else would trace[2] him, his umbrage,[3] nothing more.

OSRIC.

Your lordship speaks most infallibly of him.

HAMLET.

The concernancy,[4] sir? why do we wrap the gentleman in our more rawer breath?[5]

OSRIC.

Sir?

HORATIO.

Is't not possible to understand in another tongue?[6] You will do't, sir, really.

HAMLET.

What imports the nomination of this gentleman?[7]

OSRIC.

Of Laertes?

HORATIO [aside to HAMLET].

His purse is empty already: all's[8] golden words are spent.

HAMLET.

Of him, sir.

OSRIC.

I know you are not ignorant—

HAMLET.

I would you did, sir; yet, in faith, if you did, it would not much approve me:[9]—well, sir.

OSRIC.

You are not ignorant of what excellence Laertes is—

HAMLET.

I dare not confess that, lest I should compare with him in excellence; but, to know a man well, were to know himself.

---

his semblable is his/mirror: to find anything like him, it is necessary to look in his mirror. [2] trace: emulate. [3] umbrage: shadow. the concernancy: the relevance; in other words, how does this concern me? [5] rawer breath: coarser speech in comparison with so exquisite a subject. [6] in another tongue: in more reasonable language. [7] What imports the nomination of this gentleman: what is the meaning behind your naming this gentleman? [8] all's: all his. it would not/much approve me: your approval of me would not matter greatly.

OSRIC.

I mean, sir, for his weapon; but in the imputation[1] laid on him by them, in his meed [2] he's unfellow'd.[3]

HAMLET.

What's his weapon?

OSRIC.

Rapier and dagger.

HAMLET.

That's two of his weapons: but, well.

OSRIC.

The king, sir, hath wager'd with him six Barbary horses: against the which he has imponed,[4] as I take it, six French rapiers and poniards, with their assigns,[5] as girdle, hangers,[6] and so: three of the carriages, in faith, are very dear to fancy,[7] very responsive to the hilts, most delicate carriages, and of very liberal conceit.[8]

HAMLET.

What call you the carriages?

HORATIO [aside to HAMLET].

I knew you must be edified by the margent[9] ere you had done.

OSRIC.

The carriages, sir, are the hangers.

HAMLET.

The phrase would be more german[10] to the matter, if we could carry cannon by our sides: I would it might be hangers till then. But, on: six Barbary horses against six French swords, their assigns, and three liberal-conceited carriages; that's the French bet against the Danish. Why is this 'imponed,' as you call it?

OSRIC.

The king, sir, hath laid,[11] that in a dozen passes between

---

[1] imputation: reputation. [2] meed: merits. [3] unfellow'd: unequaled. [4] imponed: staked. [5] assigns: accessories. [6] girdle, hangers: sword belt and straps from which the weapon was hung. [7] very dear to fancy: elaborately designed. [8] of very liberal conceit: showing great imagination. [9] margent: that is, it would require marginal notes to explain Osric's flowery language. [10] german: germane; appropriate. [11] laid: bet.

ourself and him, he shall not exceed you three hits: he hath
aid on twelve for nine; and it would come to immediate
rial, if your lordship would vouchsafe the answer.[1]

HAMLET.

How if I answer no?

OSRIC.

mean, my lord, the opposition of your person in trial.

HAMLET.

ir, I will walk here in the hall: if it please his majesty, 'tis the
reathing time of day with me;[2] let the foils be brought, the
entleman willing, and the king hold his purpose, I will win
or him an I can; if not, I will gain nothing but my shame and
he odd hits.

OSRIC.

hall I re-deliver you e'en so?[3]

HAMLET.

o this effect, sir; after what flourish your nature will.

OSRIC.

commend my duty to your lordship.

HAMLET.

ours, yours. [*Exit* OSRIC.]—He does well to commend it
imself; there are no tongues else for's turn.[4]

HORATIO.

his lapwing runs away with the shell on his head.[5]

HAMLET.

Ie did comply with his dug,[6] before he suckt it. Thus has

---

would vouchsafe the answer: that is, guarantee acceptance of
he challenge. [2] the breathing time of day with me: my time for
elaxation. [3] re-deliver you e'en so: take back your message to this
ffect. [4] for's turn: to do it the way he will. [5] This lapwing runs
way with the shell on his head: this fellow, like the lapwing, is in
great hurry, (the lapwing starts to run about before it is fully
atched). [6] He did comply with his dug: literally, he begged the
reast's pardon; in other words, he observed the amenities.

he—and many more of the same bevy, that I know the drossy[1]
age dotes on—only got the tune of the time, and outward
habit of encounter;[2] a kind of yesty[3] collection, which carried
them through and through the most fann'd and winnow'd[4]
opinions; and do but blow them to their trial, the bubbles are
out.

Enter a LORD.

LORD.

My lord, his majesty commended him to you by young Osric,
who brings back to him, that you attend him in the hall: he
sends to know if your pleasure hold to play[5] with Laertes, or
that you will take longer time.

HAMLET.

I am constant to my purposes; they follow the king's pleasure:
if his fitness speaks, mine is ready; now or whensoever, provided I be so able as now.

LORD.

The king and queen and all are coming down.

HAMLET.

In happy time.

LORD.

The queen desires you to use some gentle entertainment[6] to
Laertes before you fall to play.

HAMLET.

She well instructs me.   [*Exit* LORD.

HORATIO.

You will lose this wager, my lord.

HAMLET.

I do not think so; since he went into France, I have been in
continual practice; I shall win at the odds. But thou wouldst
not think how ill all's here about my heart: but it is no matter.

---

[1] drossy: worthless; sorry. [2] outward, habit of encounter: formal
manners and phrases of the day. [3] yesty: yeasty; frothy. [4] fann'd
and winnow'd: selected, as grain is separated from the chaff.
[5] if your pleasure hold to play: if you are ready to begin the
contest. [6] use some gentle entertainment: that is, greet him
courteously.

HORATIO.

Nay, good my lord,—

HAMLET.

It is but foolery;[1] but it is such a kind of gain-giving[2] as
would perhaps trouble a woman.

HORATIO.

If your mind dislike any thing, obey it: I will forestall their
repair[3] hither, and say you are not fit.

HAMLET.

Not a whit, we defy augury:[4] there's a special providence in
the fall of a sparrow. If it be now, 'tis not to come; if it be not
to come, it will be now; if it be not now, yet it will come: the
readiness is all: since no man knows aught of what he leaves,
what is't to leave betimes? Let be.

Enter KING, QUEEN, LAERTES, LORDS, OSRIC, *and* ATTENDANTS
  with foils and gauntlets: a table and flagons of wine on it.

KING.

Come, Hamlet, come, and take this hand from me.

          [*The* KING *puts* LAERTES' *hand into* HAMLET'S.

HAMLET.

Give me your pardon, sir: I've done you wrong;
But pardon't, as you are a gentleman.
This presence[5] knows,
And you must needs have heard, how I am punisht
With sore distraction. What I have done,
That might your nature, honour, and exception
Roughly awake, I here proclaim was madness.
Was't Hamlet wrong'd Laertes? Never Hamlet:
If Hamlet from himself be ta'en away,

---

[1] foolery: foolishness.
[2] gain-giving: misgiving.
[3] repair: coming.
[4] augury: omens.
[5] this presence: this royal audience.

And when he's not himself does wrong Laertes,
Then Hamlet does it not, Hamlet denies it.
Who does it, then? His madness: if't be so,
Hamlet is of the faction that is wrong'd;
His madness is poor Hamlet's enemy.
Sir, in this audience,
Let my disclaiming from a purposed evil
Free me so far in your most generous thoughts,
That I have shot mine arrow o'er the house,
And hurt my brother.

    LAERTES.

                I am satisfied in nature,[1]
Whose motive, in this case, should stir me most
To my revenge: but in my terms of honour
I stand aloof; and will no reconcilement
Till by some elder masters, of known honour,
I have a voice and precedent of peace,
To keep my name ungored.[2] But till that time
I do receive your offer'd love like love,
And will not wrong it. '

    HAMLET.

                I embrace it freely;
And will this brother's wager frankly play.—
Give us the foils.—Come on.

    LAERTES.

                Come, one for me.

    HAMLET.

I'll be your foil, Laertes: in mine ignorance
Your skill shall, like a star i'th'darkest night,
Stick fiery off indeed.[3]

    LAERTES.

                You mock me, sir.

---

[1] in nature: as far as my personal feelings are concerned.
[2] ungored: unstained.
[3] Stick fiery off indeed: stand out all the more brightly by contrast.

HAMLET.

No, by this hand.

KING.

Give them the foils, young Osric.—Cousin Hamlet,
You know the wager?

HAMLET.

               Very well, my lord;
Your Grace hath laid the odds o'th'weaker side.

KING.

I do not fear it; I have seen you both:
But since he is better'd, we have therefore odds.

LAERTES.

This is too heavy, let me see another.

HAMLET.

This likes me well. These foils have all a length?[1]

                            [They prepare to play

OSRIC.

Ay, my good lord.

KING.

Set me the stoops of wine upon that table.—
If Hamlet give the first or second hit,
Or quit in answer of the third exchange,
Let all the battlements their ordance[2] fire;
The king shall drink to Hamlet's better breath;[3]
And in the cup an union[4] shall he throw,
Richer than that which four successive kings
In Denmark's crown have worn. Give me the cups;
And let the kettle[5] to the trumpet speak,
The trumpet to the cannoneer without,
The cannons to the heavens, the heaven to earth,
'Now the king drinks to Hamlet.'—Come, begin;
And you, the judges, bear a wary eye.

---

[1] have all a length: are all the same length.
[2] ordnance: cannon.
[3] better breath: better health; to his winning the contest.
[4] union: a large and perfect pearl.
[5] kettle: kettledrum.

HAMLET.
Come on, sir.

LAERTES.
Come, my lord.   [*They play.*

HAMLET.
One.

LAERTES.
No.

HAMLET.
Judgement.

OSRIC.
A hit, a very palpable hit.

LAERTES.
Well;—again.

KING.
Stay; give me drink.—Hamlet, this pearl is thine;
Here's to thy health.

[*Trumpets sound, and shot goes off.*
Give him the cup.

HAMLET.
I'll play this bout first; set it by awhile.—
Come.—[*They play.*] Another hit; what say you?

LAERTES.
A touch, a touch, I do confess.

KING.
Our son shall win.

QUEEN.
He's fat, and scant of breath.
Here, Hamlet, take my napkin, rub thy brows:
The queen carouses[1] to thy fortune, Hamlet.

HAMLET.
Good madam!

---

[1] carouses: drinks.

KING.

Gertrude, do not drink.

QUEEN.

I will, my lord; I pray you, pardon me.   [*Drinks.*

KING [*aside*].

It is the poison'd cup; it is too late.

HAMLET.

I dare not drink yet, madam; by and by.

QUEEN.

Come, let me wipe thy face.

LAERTES.

My lord, I'll hit him now.

KING.

I do not think't.

LAERTES [*aside*].

And yet 'tis almost 'gainst my conscience.

HAMLET.

Come, for the third, Laertes: you but dally;
I pray you, pass with your best violence;
I am afeared you make a wanton of me.[1]

LAERTES.

Say you so? come on.   [*They play.*

OSRIC.

Nothing, neither way.

LAERTES.

Have at you now!

[LAERTES *wounds* HAMLET; *then, in scuffling they change
        rapiers, and* HAMLET *wounds* LAERTES.

KING.

Part them; they are incensed.

HAMLET.

Nay, come, again.   [*The* QUEEN *falls.*

---

[1] make a wanton of me: treat me as a child; trifle with me.

OSRIC.

Look to the queen there, ho!

HORATIO.

They bleed on both sides.—How is it, my lord?

OSRIC.

How is't, Laertes?

LAERTES.

Why, as a woodcock to mine own springe,[1] Osric; I am justly
kill'd with mine own treachery.

HAMLET.

How does the queen?

KING.

She swounds[2] to see them bleed.

QUEEN.

No, no, the drink, the drink,—O my dear Hamlet,—
The drink, the drink!—I am poison'd.   [*Dies.*

HAMLET.

O villainy!—Ho! let the door be lockt:
Treachery! seek it out.   [LAERTES *falls.*

LAERTES.

It is here, Hamlet: Hamlet, thou art slain;
No medicine in the world can do thee good,
In thee there is not half an hour of life;
The treacherous instrument is in thy hand,
Unbated and envenom'd: the foul practice[3]
Hath turn'd itself on me; lo, here I lie,
Never to rise again: thy mother's poison'd:—
I can no more:—the king, the king's to blame.

HAMLET.

The point envenom'd too!—
Then, venom, to thy work.   [*Stabs the* KING.

ALL.

Treason! treason!

---

[1] springe: snare.
[2] swounds: swoons; faints.
[3] practice: plot.

KING.

O, yet defend me, friends; I am but hurt.

HAMLET.

Here, thou incestuous, murderous, damned Dane,
Drink off this potion:—is thy union here?
Follow my mother.   [KING *dies*.

LAERTES.

He is justly served;
It is a poison temper'd [1] by himself.—
Exchange forgiveness with me, noble Hamlet:
Mine and my father's death come not upon thee.
Nor thine on me!   [*Dies*.

HAMLET.

Heaven make thee free of it! I follow thee.—
I am dead, Horatio.—Wretched queen, adieu!—
You that look pale and tremble at this chance,[2]
That are but mutes or audience to this act,
Had I but time,— as this fell sergeant, death,
Is strict in his arrest,—O, I could tell you,—
But let it be.—Horatio, I am dead;
Thou livest; report me and my cause aright
To the unsatisfied.

HORATIO.

Never believe it:
I am more an antique Rôman[3] than a Dane:
Here's yet some liquor left.

HAMLET.

As th'art a man,
Give me the cup: let go; by heaven, I'll have't.
O good Horatio, what a wounded name,
Things standing thus unknown, shall live behind me!

---

temper'd: prepared; mixed.
chance: mischance.
antique Roman: an allusion to the practice of ancient Romans
to commit suicide.

If thou didst ever hold me in thy heart,
Absent thee from felicity awhile,
And in this harsh world draw thy breath in pain,
To tell my story. [*March afar off, and shot within.*
           What warlike noise is this?

    OSRIC.

Young Fortinbras, with conquest[1] come from Poland,
To the ambassadors of England gives
This warlike volley.

    HAMLET.

           O, I die, Horatio;
The potent poison quite o'er-crows[2] my spirit:
I cannot live to hear the news from England;
But I do prophesy th'election lights[3]
On Fortinbras: he has my dying voice;
So tell him, with the occurrents,[4] more and less,
Which have solicited[5]—the rest is silence.   [*Dies.*

    HORATIO.

Now cracks a noble heart.—Good night, sweet prince;
And flights of angels sing thee to thy rest!—
Why does the drum come hither?   [*March within.*
Enter FORTINBRAS *and the English* AMBASSADORS, *with drum,*
         colours, and ATTENDANTS.

    FORTINBRAS.

Where is this sight?

    HORATIO.

           What is it ye would see?
If aught of woe or wonder, cease your search.

    FORTINBRAS.

This quarry[6] cries on[7] havoc.[8]—O proud Death,
What feast is toward[9] in thine eternal cell,

---

[1] **with conquest**: victorious. [2] **o'er-crows**: overcomes. [3] **lights**: falls upon. [4] **occurents**: occurences. [5] **solicited**: brought about the event. [6] **quarry**: pile of dead game (a hunting term). [7] **cries on**: indicates [8] **havoc**: the battle cry when no quarter was to be given: therefore ruthless or indiscriminate slaughter. [9] **is toward**: is in preparation

That thou so many princes at a shot
So bloodily hast struck?

  FIRST AMBASSADOR.

       The sight is dismal;
And our affairs from England come too late:
The ears are senseless that should give us hearing,
To tell him his commandment is fulfill'd,
That Rosencrantz and Guildenstern are dead:
Where should we have our thanks?

  HORATIO.

        Not from his mouth.
Had it th'ability of life to thank you:
He never gave commandment for their death.
But since, so jump upon this bloody question,[1]
You from the Polack wars, and you from England,
Are here arrived, give order that these bodies
High on a stage be placed to the view;
And let me speak to th'yet unknowing world
How these things came about: so shall you hear
Of carnal, bloody, and unnatural acts;
Of accidental judgements, casual slaughters;
Of deaths put on by cunning and forced cause;
And, in this upshot, purposes mistook
Faln on the inventors' heads: all this can I
Truly deliver.

  FORTINBRAS.

    Let us haste to hear it,
And call the noblest to the audience.
For me, with sorrow I embrace my fortune:
I have some rights of memory in this kingdom,
Which now to claim my vantage doth invite me.

---

[1] so jump upon this bloody question: upon the very heels of these bloody events.

HORATIO.

Of that I shall have also cause to speak,
And from his mouth whose voice will draw on more:
But let this same be presently perform'd,
Even while men's minds are wild; lest more mischance,
On plots and errors, happen.

FORTINBRAS.

                  Let four captains
Bear Hamlet, like a soldier, to the stage;
For he was likely, had he been put on[1]
To have proved most royally:[2] and, for his passage,[3]
The soldiers' music and the rites of war
Speak loudly for him.—
Take up the bodies:—such a sight as this
Becomes the field, but here shows much amiss.—
Go, bid the soldiers shoot.

[A dead march. Exeunt, bearing off the dead bodies; after
    which a peal of ordnance is shot off.

---

[1] put on: put to the test; that is, crowned king.
[2] To have proved most royally: to have proved himself a just and
honored king.
[3] his passage: his passing.

THE AIRMONT SHAKESPEARE LIBRARY

All titles available at 50¢ each

Killed

Polonius – stabbed by Hamlet

Ophilia – suicide

~~Kon~~ Queen – drinks poisa cup

King – stabbed by Hamlet

Laertes – stabbed by Hamlet

Hamlet – stabbed by Laertes